Walking on Water

Walking On Water

Sermons on the Miracles of Jesus

James O. Gilliom

Abingdon Press
Nashville

WALKING ON WATER: SERMONS ON THE MIRACLES OF JESUS

Copyright © 1995 by Abingdon Press

' All rights reserved.

This book is printed on recycled, acid-free paper.

Library of Congress Cataloging-in-Publication Data

Gilliom, James O.
    Walking on water: sermons on the miracles of Jesus/James O.
Gilliom.
        p.   cm.—(Protestant pulpit exchange)
    ISBN 0-687-01138-8 (pbk.: alk. paper)
    1. Jesus Christ—Miracles—Sermons.   2. Sermons, American.
I. Title.   II. Series.
BT366.G55   1995
232.9'55—dc20   95-5371
                                                                                CIP

Scripture quotations, except for brief paraphrases or unless otherwise noted, are from the New Revised Standard Version Bible, copyright 1989 by the Division of Christian Education of the National Council of the Churches of Christ in the USA. Used by permission.

Those noted RSV are from the Revised Standard Version of the Bible, copyright 1946, 1952, 1971 by the Division of Christian Education of the National Council of Churches of Christ in the USA. Used by permission.

Those noted Phillips are from J. B. Phillips, *The New Testament in Modern English* (Macmillan, 1972), copyright © J. B. Phillips 1958, 1959, 1960, 1972.

Those noted GNB are from the *Good News Bible*—Old Testament: Copyright © American Bible Society 1976; New Testament: Copyright © American Bible Society 1966, 1971, 1976.

Those noted NEB are from *The New English Bible*. © The Delegates of the Oxford University Press and The Syndics of the Cambridge University Press 1961, 1970. Reprinted by permission.

Those noted NASB are from the New American Standard Bible, © The Lockman Foundation 1960, 1962, 1968, 1971, 1972, 1973, 1975, 1977.

Those noted NJB are from the New Jerusalem Bible, copyright © 1985 by Darton, Longman & Todd, Ltd., and Doubleday & Co., Inc.

Those noted KJV are from the King James Version of the Bible.

"Matthew VIII, 28ff" is from *Walking to Sleep: New Poems and Translations,* copyright © 1969 by Richard Wilbur, reprinted by permission of Harcourt Brace & Company, and Faber and Faber Ltd.

95 96 97 98 99 00 01 02 03 04—10 9 8 7 6 5 4 3 2 1

MANUFACTURED IN THE UNITED STATES OF AMERICA

Contents

Introduction

My sermons are usually based on the Revised Common Lectionary readings. I find study of the lectionary scriptures an effective personal discipline. Also, the congregation is protected from overuse of my favorite passages and is likely to receive more of the essential themes of our faith.

But special series built on themes also have their place, and one of my favorite series subjects is the stories of Jesus' miracles. Why? I think that in large part it is because of the powerful message they communicate that change is possible with the help of a loving God. Two parts of the worship liturgy that have always had special meaning for me are the assurance of God's love following the confession of sin, and the benediction. The assurance promises the miracle of release from past sins, mistakes, grievances, and tragedies and the miracle of new birth and resurrection for the future. The benediction bestows the miracle of God's blessing as we reenter the world as changed and yet-to-be changed persons. The benediction that I have used for years is adapted from Ephesians 3:20-21: "Now to that God who through the power at work within us is able to accomplish abundantly far more than all we can ask or imagine be all glory in the church and throughout all God's world, in Jesus' name. Amen."

Change, miraculous change beyond our own power or even imagination, is possible with God's help. And that seems to me to be the homiletical point of the miracle stories.

Jesus' miracles, of course, have been interpreted in different ways. Even the Gospel writers were not united in their descriptions, the dissimilar resurrection stories being the foremost example. The Gospel of John refers to Jesus' miracles as "signs," emphasizing that they were not tricks or wonders to astound, but signs pointing to God's special presence in Jesus. The story of turning the water into wine concludes: "Jesus did this, the first of his signs, in Cana of Galilee, and revealed his glory; and his disciples believed in him" (John 2:11). But Matthew's story of Jesus' time alone in the wilderness after his baptism suggests that performing miracles even as "signs" was a temptation of the devil to be resisted!

Nevertheless, can you imagine how inspiring and comforting the miracle stories were to the early Christians being persecuted? Atrocities beyond reason needed to be met with faith beyond reason, faith in a God who through such "signs" demonstrated ultimate truths and values for which even dying was worthwhile. When the ship of the church seemed ready to sink, how sustaining must have been the story of Jesus stilling the storm on the Sea of Galilee. I suspect that little time was spent by conservatives or liberals in the early Church arguing about the historical accuracy of the miracles or the literalism with which they were to be taken. The spiritual truths the stories conveyed were accurate in their experience. The miracles indeed were unforgettable "signs" of the divine presence in Jesus that made him the living Christ now known within them. How the early Christians understood the physics of the miracles could vary, but their certainty of the spiritual teachings of the miracles would be passed on from generation to generation.

The miracles of Jesus are generally of three types. There are the *spiritual* miracles, such as the changing of Zacchaeus from mean and selfish to a generous man who helps the poor.

There are the *nature* miracles. These include the changing of water into wine at Cana, and the stilling of the storm on the Sea of Galilee.

Then there are many *healing* miracles, which can be subdivided into two groups: mental and physical. Mental healings include that of the demoniac in the land of the Gerasenes. Physical healings include that of the paralytic who rose, picked up his bed, and walked home.

The miracle stories included in this series are categorized as miracles of healing, miracles beyond nature, and miracles of the spirit. Miracles of healing include the two types of healings. For miracles beyond nature I have included stories of Jesus' virgin birth and

8

his resurrection. Both share wide variances in their earliest telling and in their interpretations today, and both unforgettably convey gospel truths. Miracles of the spirit are signs of how the human spirit can be enlivened by the acceptance of God's Spirit, such as the Emmaus disciples making one of history's fastest U-turns from depression to action on Easter afternoon, and Jesus' miraculous ability to conquer the evil and hatred in the world around him with his overcoming love. Although not based on any of Jesus' miracles, the sermon "When Miracles Fail" concerns a subject that will surely be asked about whenever a series on miracles is delivered.

We all know that the miracles have been preached in different ways—literally, allegorically, metaphorically; with triumphalism and with apology; with deathly scholasticism and with pop psychology. My preaching is based on the need of people to hear and believe in the power of God's loving and resurrecting presence in their lives. I have tried, therefore, to present the ancient miracle stories in ways that will win people to the belief that the same God whom the early Christians saw within the miracle stories, whether we take them literally or symbolically, wants also to be within us "to accomplish abundantly far more than all we can ask or imagine."

The text that guides my preaching of the miracles, and all my sermons, is Jesus' reply to those who criticized his behavior on the sabbath, "The sabbath was made for humankind, and not human-kind for the sabbath" (Mark 2:27). The miracle stories are to be used by preachers today, not for dogmatic browbeating, but to commu-nicate to people of all conditions that change is possible with the help of a loving God. To that end I pray that these sermons delivered to the people of Plymouth Congregational United Church of Christ in Des Moines, Iowa, will also minister to you.

To that great congregation, which has been the channel of numerous miracles by God in its community, its own church life, and countless personal lives (including my own), I owe inexpressible thanks; also to Jean Olson, my secretary, and Donna, my wife, both of whom have performed the miracle of transferring my handwrit-ing to the printed page; and finally to Paul Franklyn, Cynthia Gadsden, and Steven W. Cox of Abingdon Press, whose encourage-ment and counsel were essential for bringing these pages to publi-cation.

James O. Gilliom

9

Miracles Of Healing

The Paralytic on the Roof

> *"But so that you may know that the Son of Man has authority on earth to forgive sins"—he said to the paralytic—"I say to you, stand up, take your mat and go to your home."*
> *Mark 2:10-11*

How Forgiving Heals

Mark 2:1-12

The story takes place, it is commonly believed, in the Capernaum house of Simon and Andrew, which has become Jesus' home after his rejection by Nazareth, his own hometown.

Jesus has now become very popular. A large crowd fills the house and surrounds it. The Phillips translation says, "It was impossible even to get near the doorway."

Among those who cannot get in are four persons carrying a stretcher bearing their paralyzed friend. And what good friends they are. For, instead of simply accepting the disappointment of not getting in, rather than settling for the rejection, they devise an alternative plan.

A typical house of the time had an inner courtyard, which was the gathering place. This is where Jesus would have been sitting, teaching. Above the courtyard was a roof to protect from the rain and the Middle Eastern sun's heat. The roof was made of planks, about three

13

feet apart, covered with branches, dirt, and sometimes even a crop of grass.

This is what the four friends do. After wrestling the stretcher up to the roof above the courtyard where Jesus teaches, they open up a hole between the rafters, large enough to let the stretcher down with improvised ropes.

Those in the already crowded courtyard have to press back even farther to make room for the astonishing descent. And Jesus probably can't help smiling as he looks up at the audacious friends, so carefully working together, synchronizing the ropes so they won't drop the stretcher and cause even more suffering.

As a matter of fact, the scripture says that it was after "Jesus saw their faith" that he spoke to the paralytic.

One of the obvious teachings of this story is the importance of friends.

- Friends, who help move us to a new future, when we are paralyzed by life's troubles and fears.
- Friends, who encourage and lift us up, when we cannot rise by ourselves.
- Friends, who apply their ingenuity and tenacity, when we are ready to surrender.
- Friends, who open up holes in life's roofs for us, and enable us to see new opportunities.

"When Jesus saw their faith," Mark says, he spoke to the one who was paralyzed.

And then the healing miracle is described.

Jesus says to the one who is paralyzed, "Son, your sins are forgiven."

Whoa! Wait a minute! What's going on here? "Your sins are forgiven." We want a healing, not absolution!

Or does Jesus know something that others don't? Has he heard of this case? Maybe Simon told him. Or maybe he can tell just by looking in the paralytic's eyes that what he is crippled by is guilt.

Some religious scribes are present, the protectors of orthodoxy whatever the human cost. They protest: "Why does this fellow speak in this way? It is blasphemy! Who can forgive sins but God alone?" (Mark 2:7).

To which Jesus replies, "Why do you raise such questions in your hearts? Which is easier, to say to the paralytic, 'Your sins are forgiven,' or to say, 'Stand up and take your mat and walk'?"

Isn't that the truth? Physical illness can often be dealt with so much more easily than mental and spiritual illness.

"But," says Jesus, "that you may know that the Son of Man has authority on earth to forgive sins . . . I say to you, stand up, take your mat and go to your home."

The story concludes, according to the Phillips translation:

> At once the man sprang to his feet, picked up his bed and walked off in full view of them all. Everyone was amazed, praised God and said, "We have never seen anything like this before."

And what can we learn today from the story? Aside from the importance of letting friends help us, I think it is this: The Christian faith recognizes with compassion the power of guilt to cripple. And it offers another power—the power of forgiveness to heal.

> *The Christian faith recognizes with compassion the power of forgiveness to heal.*

Guilt is defined by Webster as "a painful feeling of self-reproach from a belief that one has done something wrong or immoral."

Leslie Weatherhead, in his classic study *Psychology, Religion and Healing,* says there are three kinds of guilt.

The first is *normal guilt.* Normal guilt is good and necessary, both for our personal well-being and for society's. This is that sense of conscience which, like pain, first warns us that something is wrong. Sociologist Amitai Etzioni, while teaching at Harvard Business School, had a piece published in the *New York Times.* It was titled "Say 'I'm Sorry' Like a Man." In it he bemoaned the lack of normal guilt among so many national figures. It has been called "the sleaze factor" and is exemplified by public figures who betray public trust and show no remorse.

Second, Weatherhead says there is *exaggerated conscience guilt.* By this is meant such an overwhelming sense of shame after something has happened that feelings of guilt are exaggerated out of proportion.

15

This is sometimes the case with persons who have recently divorced. The sense of failure is so great that it triggers a morose period of depressing self-doubt and innate worthlessness. Realistic evaluation, of what may have become a destructive relationship beyond reasonable expectation of salvaging, tapers to a weak and distant voice, while the voice of guilt shouts, "Failure, failure!" Exaggerated conscience guilt, whatever the cause, is one of our most common maladies, especially—I must say—among religiously sensitive perfectionists. As Ogden Nash put it, there are those

> Who are very resourceful
> At being remorseful.

And the third kind of guilt named is *repressed guilt*. In this case, past events are so objectionable that feelings of guilt have been repressed into the unconscious. An incident may even be forgotten so far as the conscious mind admits, but the guilt keeps manifesting itself in abnormal behavior. This is often the situation in cases of dysfunctional adults with histories of molestation or abuse as children. Those of you who have read Jane Smiley's Pulitzer Prize–winning novel *A Thousand Acres* will recall that repressed guilt from childhood sexual abuse was one of the main themes. Repressed guilt almost always needs special therapy, if it is to lose its diabolical power to cripple life.

Now, let's head back toward the miracle story by way of the route of what are called four steps in the treatment of guilt, also as outlined by Weatherhead.

First, *face it*. Stop avoiding what is making you feel guilty. Its appetite for your energy is voracious. It can consume you if its existence is denied. Sharing your struggle with good friends or a support group, like the four friends of the paralytic, may help you face the truth. Writer John Updike says, "We take our bearings, daily, from others. To be sane is to a great extent, to be sociable."

---

*Stop avoiding what is making you feel guilty.
It can consume you if its existence is denied.*

Second, *confess it.* Get it out. Articulate it. Name it. Demons traditionally lose their power when they are named. This is the truth that is behind all psychotherapy and the Prayer of Confession: acknowledgment of our transgressions, our iniquities. Or, as is often the case with persons who suffer from repressed guilt from early sexual abuse, acknowledge and name the evil in others, the suppression of which can continue to cripple for years. Psychologist William James called these acknowledgments "the exteriorizing of our rottenness."

Third, *make reparation.* If an object is stolen, return it. If a person is unjustly offended, apologize. If a lie is spoken, retract it. If justice has been denied, work for it. Etzioni says:

> Nobody can lead a blame-free life. But if we do violate the law or ethical standards, we can still straighten things out and avoid further harm. We must acknowledge our wrongs, make amends to those we injured and to the community whose legal and moral precepts we undermined.

And now we are back to the climax of the miracle, for the fourth step in the treatment of guilt is *acceptance of God's forgiveness.* Weatherhead says:

> Here, of course, we come to the very heart of the matter. The forgiveness of God, in my opinion, is the most powerful therapeutic idea in the world. If a person really believes that God has forgiven, then the burden of guilt and the fear at the heart of it disappear.

Believe you are forgiven. Get up and move on to your new life with the power of God's Holy Spirit!

And thus we have our assurance of God's love through prayers such as this one from the *Book of Worship* of the United Church of Christ:

> God hears the confession of our hearts and lips.
> Through Jesus Christ we are forgiven all our sins, and by the Holy Spirit we are empowered for new life. . . . Believe the good news of Jesus Christ.

Believe you are forgiven. Stop replaying old guilt tapes. Get up and move on to your new life with the power of God's Holy Spirit!

- Jeremiah wrote: Thus says the Lord, "I will forgive their iniquity, and remember their sin no more." (31:34)
- Isaiah wrote: "O Lord, . . . you have cast all my sins behind your back." (38:16-17)
- Paul wrote: Love "does not rejoice in wrongdoing." (1 Cor. 13:6)
- And Jesus said: "Your sins are forgiven. . . . I say to you, stand up, take your mat and go to your home." (Mark 2:9-11)

We do not have Christ with us in the physical sense that he was present in Capernaum. But his recognition of someone's genuinely needing help in ridding self of the ravages of guilt and his confidence in the possibility of new life, are as valid today as they were then.

Whether you identify with the paralytic, the friends, or even the Christ, the agent of God's healing, may you know the strength and joy of the miraculous healing power of forgiveness, both as giver and as receiver of the liberation from guilt paralysis.

If you do, then you too will be "amazed" and exclaim, "We never saw anything like this!" Amen.

> *They came to Jesus and saw the demoniac sitting there, clothed and in his right mind, the very man who had had the legion. Mark 5:15*

Who's Running Your Life?

Mark 5:1-20

*D*emonism is the belief that your life is controlled by superhuman and destructive powers outside your own will.

After comedian Flip Wilson's character Geraldine used to admit to some dastardly act, she would plead, "But the devil made me do it!" That is one form of demonism.

Some people believe in demonism's near relative, fatalism, which also says that our lives are controlled by powers outside our wills, and before which we are helpless. "His or her number was up" is a common expression of fatalism.

Some religious people believe that God causes everything that happens to them. "It is the will of God" is for them the ultimate expression of pietism. Not accident, not willful human evil, not human ignorance, but the will of God is the source of life's troubles.

And all such philosophies are ways of saying that in the final word, people are not able to run their own lives. Other powers have taken control. We are not decision makers, but victims. Our goal is not redemption and re-creation, but rather—afraid of experiencing more pain in a hostile world beyond our powers—surrender and mere survival.

The demoniac in this scripture passage is a man who has finally gone mad in the face of it all.

We don't know what dreams for the future the imagination of his mind once harbored. We don't know what "slings and arrows of outrageous fortune" have so wounded him.

All we know is that the world has become too much for him. He has lost all resilience to cope with life's stresses and strains. And in response to the destructiveness of the world around him, he has become self-destructive.

At first his community tries to control him. In those days, before sedatives and other mind-controlling drugs, that meant binding him with fetters around his ankles and chains around his wrists. That failing—he breaks them both and "no one had the strength to subdue him"—they banish him. He now lives—shouting, crying, and bruising himself—in a cemetery among the tombs.

The chief symbol of his sorry condition, though, is that his ego has become so diminished that he believes he has no power anymore in the running of his own life. The demons have taken over. He is their victim. And when Jesus asks, "What is your name?" he answers, "My name is Legion; for we are many."

Jesus asks, "What is your name?" He answers, "My name is Legion; for we are many."

A legion was a Roman measure usually meaning four to six thousand soldiers. What chance does one fragile human ego have against four to six thousand demons?

But then the miracle takes place.

The Incarnation, that embodiment of the God-who-is-love, the one we call the Christ, sees something in the man that is worth redeeming and re-creating.

> *The one we call the Christ sees something in the demoniac that is worth redeeming and re-creating.*

Nearby there is a large herd of swine, about two thousand. Jesus orders the demons to leave the poor man alone, and instead to enter the swine. As indication of the demons' power, the swine then go crazy, rushing down a steep bank into the sea, where they drown; while the man, free of his demons, now sits peacefully, "clothed and in his right mind, the very man who had had the legion."

It is the miracle that inspired John Greenleaf Whittier to write:

> Dear Lord and Father of mankind,
>   forgive our foolish ways;
>   reclothe us in our rightful mind . . .
>   Take from our souls the strain and stress,
>   and let our ordered lives confess
>   the beauty of thy peace.

Are there still demons working today? Do demons still possess us and try to control our lives?

You could say that demons possess a teenager when that legion called "peer pressure" becomes destructive during those critical years of value-and-life formation.

You could say that demons possess anyone who suspends individual judgment and becomes superficial and mean-spirited in order to fit in with a crowd (or legion). Friedrich Nietzsche, in his book *Human, All Too Human,* describes the moral seductiveness and sly coercion of social gatherings: "Why do we feel pangs of conscience after ordinary parties? Because we have taken important matters lightly; because we have discussed people with less than complete loyalty, or because we were silent when we should have spoken; because we behaved at the party as if we belonged to it."

You could say that demons possess politicians who listen to the legion of the polls more than to their own principles.

You could say that demons possess TV evangelists who become manipulators for a legion of personal gains rather than ministers for the good of others.

21

You could say that demons possess parents who abdicate family responsibilities at home to win a legion of advancements in the marketplace.

You could say that demons possess the philandering husband or wife who cannot resist the legion of temptation's whispers.

You could say that demons possess any who are so compulsive about competing and succeeding that they sacrifice their own beings to win the favor of those legions. That sometimes sardonic philosopher of the book of Ecclesiastes wrote:

> I have also learned why people work so hard to succeed: it is because they envy the things their neighbors have. But it is useless. It is like chasing the wind. They say that one would be a fool to fold his or her hands and let self starve to death. Maybe so, but it is better to have only a little, with peace of mind, than be busy all the time with both hands, trying to catch the wind. (4:4-6, GNB adapted)

You could say that demons possess all whose driving force of life is greed. And that is the point, I think, of this curious miracle story's next twist.

Are the neighbors of the healed man pleased with his cure? Is his community grateful that he now has a new chance to rebuild his life? Do they welcome the "Miracle in the Cemetery"?

The answer to every question is no.

They would prefer, rather than rid the man of his demons, to have their swine returned, so they can sell them at a good market price next month. So Mark reports, "Those who had seen what had happened to the demoniac and to the swine reported it. Then they began to beg Jesus to leave their neighborhood."

Pulitzer Prize–winning poet Richard Wilbur wrote a poem about today's miracle story. It is this convolution of values, of possessions over people, that he emphasizes.

> Rabbi, we Gadarenes
> Are not ascetics; we are fond of wealth and possessions.
> Love, as you call it, we obviate by means
> Of the planned release of aggressions.
> We have deep faith in prosperity.
> Soon, it is hoped, we will reach our full potential.
> In the light of our gross product, the practice of charity
> Is palpably inessential.
> It is true that we go insane;
> That for no good reason we are possessed by devils;

22

That we suffer, despite the amenities which obtain
At all but the lowest levels.
We shall not, however, resign
Our trust in the high-heaped table and the full trough.
If you cannot cure us without destroying our swine,
We had rather you shoved off.

And how do you and I avoid surrendering our lives to the legion of demons that would like to control us, how avoid telling Jesus to "shove off" from our lives, to leave our neighborhood?

> *How do you and I keep from surrendering our lives to the legion of demons that would like to control us?*

Two very simple beginnings: Remember *who* you are; remember *whose* you are.

While I sat for hours in the hospital with my slowly dying father, the demons of depression were beginning to organize in legions within me. How depressing it was to think of the loss of this good and simple man's gifts to the world, as a tube feeder and stomach pump delayed the inevitable.

I took a lunch break to eat in the hospital cafeteria, glad that I was just another anonymous tray-pusher in a distant town. Depression thrives on self-absorption.

And then I was suddenly jolted when the server across the counter asked, "Isn't Bill Gilliom your father?"

"Yes," I replied. "How did you know?"

"Oh my, you've got that Gilliom look. You're Bill's boy all right."

I found myself standing straighter. I remembered who I was.

I don't belong to any legions. I am "Bill's boy." And I have a great heritage to continue.

In my last church in Upper Montclair, New Jersey, I had the privilege of being the pastor of Robert Moss, then president of the United Church of Christ. I was with Bob and his wife, Junia, when they were told that his cancer would take him in about six weeks.

Bob asked me, when I next came, to bring the Heidelberg Catechism for his devotional reading. Returning, I handed it to him.

He held it with both hands, but recited the first question and answer from memory.

> What is thy only comfort in life and death?
> That I, with body and soul, both in life and death, am not my own, but belong to my faithful Saviour Jesus Christ.

The miracle story ends with Jesus saying to the restored man, "Go home to your friends," (Remember who you are) "and tell them how much the Lord has done for you, and what mercy he has shown you" (Remember whose you are).

"And he went away and began to proclaim in the Decapolis how much Jesus had done for him; and everyone was amazed." Amen.

Bartimaeus, the Blind Beggar

Jesus stood still and said, "Call him here." . . .
Then Jesus said to him, "What do you want me
to do for you?" Mark 10:49, 51

Who Can See?

Mark 10:46-52

*T*his miracle story features the juxtaposition of Jesus and Bartimaeus. They could not have been more different.

Bartimaeus is just another insignificant beggar. Jesus is the Christ, the chosen one.

Bartimaeus is blind, lives in a world of darkness. Jesus sees, with even more appreciation than most people, the lilies of the field and the birds of the air; he is called "the light of the world."

Bartimaeus is considered a bother and is rejected by the crowd. Jesus is served by his disciples, who have to clear a way through the crowd that clamors to touch him.

For Bartimaeus, each day is the dead-end same, as it was for Shakespeare's Macbeth:

> Tomorrow, and tomorrow, and tomorrow,
> Creeps in this petty pace from day to day,
> To the last syllable of recorded time.

For Jesus, the week ahead will bring the exciting testing of his lifelong mission, as he moves toward the climax in Jerusalem, only fifteen miles away.

Chances were that they would never meet, or at least know it. "Out of sight, out of mind." Jesus was certainly out of blind Bartimaeus' sight. You would think that Bartimaeus would be out of Jesus' preoccupied mind.

But it is first Bartimaeus who will not let it be so. For though he has lost his sight, he has certainly not lost his voice. Astounding everyone around him, he makes himself heard over all the other excited crowd noises, shouting out: "Jesus, Son of David, have mercy on me!"

Different translations report the crowd's response:

"Many sternly ordered him to be quiet." (NRSV)
"Many rebuked him, telling him to be silent." (RSV)
"Many scolded him . . ." (GNB)
"Many of the people told him sharply to keep quiet." (Phillips)
" 'Shut up!' some of the people yelled at him." (TLB)

And then:

"But he cried out even more loudly,
'Son of David, have mercy on me!'" (NRSV)

What I want to suggest to you now is that in this ancient story, not one but three miracles happen.

And the first, and perhaps most important, is that "Jesus stopped." The New Revised Standard Version has it, "Jesus stood still."

That's all. That's a miracle. *Jesus stopped!*

With the momentum of history pushing him forward, with so much work to be done, with excitement building for a victory within grasp, with murmurs of approval and cheers of adulation feeding his ego and propelling him on—"Jesus stopped."

He revised his agenda. He halted his parade. His values so differed from those of the crowd that smiled at him while yelling at Bartimaeus, "Shut up!" that he simply had to set himself apart. So, "Jesus stopped."

And what that says to me is that when you and I catch ourselves getting carried away by values not our own, but that are crowd-pleasing; when you and I forget who we are and what we believe for the sweet taste of immediate gratification; when even career advancement and public esteem begin to control our decisions; when you and I are too busy to love people; then you and I had better learn to perform the miracle in our lives that Jesus performed in Jericho: "Jesus stopped."

Attorney Roy Cohn was a boy wonder. He had degrees from Columbia College and Columbia Law School by the time he was twenty. In 1948 he became an assistant U.S. Attorney, and he was only twenty-three when he helped prosecute Julius and Ethel Rosenberg. Achieving fame as chief counsel for Senator Joseph McCarthy, Cohn from then on became primarily known for his deceit and self-aggrandizement. For twenty years the Internal Revenue Service pursued Cohn for tax evasion. The New York State Supreme Court lifted his law license in 1986. His most sympathetic biographer (Sidney Zion, *The Autobiography of Roy Cohn*) portrays him as a rascal and master of half-truths. Another observer says that "Cohn, like a moving target, had plenty of desperate energy but no direction he could call his own." Roy Cohn, sometimes, should have stopped.

Irwin Shaw was one of the most prolific writers of modern times. His output of short stories, novels, television and movie scripts was awesome. But the quality of Shaw's work in his later years was ofttimes embarrassing in its shallowness. Reviewer Richard Schickel says in *Time* magazine, "Shaw was betrayed by his own facility. . . . There was nothing he couldn't write, so there was nothing he didn't write. Preoccupied by productivity and the demands of his life-style, he had no time left to develop the guiding vision of self and world a major novelist needs."

Irwin Shaw, sometimes, should have stopped.

> *To stop is to declare that the world around us will not provide our measures and standards.*

To stop is to declare that the world around us will not provide our measures and standards. That is what writer John Updike is saying in his autobiography, *Self-Consciousness:*

> One believes not merely to dismiss from one's life a degrading and immobilizing fear of death but to possess that Archimedean point outside the world from which to move the world. The world cannot provide its own measure and standards; these must come, strangely,

from outside, or a sorry hedonism and brute opportunism result—
a greedy panicked heart and substance abuse.

Playwright Arthur Miller says that in all his writings he seeks for
"the moment of commitment when one separates oneself from
other persons; when one chooses one's own star out of a sky full of
stars."

Some of us who have watched children grow up and leave home
and have also seen parents grow old and die or lose their minds,
have learned the importance of stopping to show love. Composers
Dick Avery and Don Marsh write:

> Love them now.
> Don't wait till they're gone away.
> Love them now, while they're around.
> Touch them, hold them, laugh and cry with them.
> Show them, tell them, don't deny them.
> Honor them, give birth and die with them now.
> Love them now before they're just a guilty memory.
> Love them now. Love them now.*

All miracles start with stopping. Indeed, the first miracle in this
story is, "Jesus stopped."

And the second is, *"Jesus asked!"*
Not told, not declared, not pronounced, not preached, not
warned, not ordered, not commanded: but asked!
Jesus asked blind Bartimaeus, "What do you want me to do for
you?"

Jesus asked blind Bartimaeus, "What do you want me to do for you?"

Is it too much to suggest that the potential for social, political,
and economic miracles which exists in Eastern Europe should be
credited in part to Mikhail Gorbachev's stopping the inexorable

---

*Copyright © 1970 by Hope Publishing Co., Carol Stream, IL 60188. All rights reserved. Used
by permission.

parade of destruction by the Communist government and asking the people, "What do you want?"

Even more thrilling to me than this one man, Bartimaeus, springing up and throwing off his mantle and gaining his sight, was the scene of multitudes in our own time rejecting oppressive world powers, leaping over walls to freedom, and seeing possibilities of new hope and joy.

And as Jesus once said of a pagan Roman centurion, "I tell you, not even in Israel have I found such faith" (Luke 7:9), I say, let us give thanks for the Soviet president who made even more miracles possible by his miracles of stopping and asking.

Jesus knew, of course, that Bartimaeus needed help. Don't we all. Robert Murphy is a professor of anthropology. When Professor Murphy was paralyzed by a tumor on his spine, he re-examined the word "disabled." He writes about it in his book *The Body Silent:*

> I was badly damaged, yet just as alive as ever, and I had to make the best of it with my remaining capabilities. It then occurred to me that this is the universal human condition. We all have to muddle through life within our limitations, and while I had certain physical handicaps, I retained many strengths. My brain was the only part of the central cortex that still worked well, but that also is where I made my living. *Disability* is an amorphous and relativistic term. Some people are unable to do what I do because they lack the mental equipment and in this sense, they are disabled and I am not. Everybody is disabled in one way or another.

That's what Jesus knew when he asked, "What do you want me to do for you?" Bartimaeus' need was for sight. Others within hearing must have wanted to shout their needs too, for certainly none was without them. That's the point of the old hymn "Amazing Grace," which confesses that in some way we are all blind and all in need of help if we are to be able truly to sing:

> I once was lost, but now am found,
> Was blind, but now I see.

Jesus stopped. Jesus asked. *Jesus healed.*

"Immediately [Bartimaeus] regained his sight and followed him on the way."

To know how Bartimaeus was healed is about as difficult as it is to know how really to help the poor, the lost, and least in our society today.

Individual, emotionally controlled, or superficial help is often misdirected and even destructive. Because of the increasing requests of people for help, congregations more and more are needing to support and work through public and other specialized church agencies that can more accurately discern true need. There is then a commensurate, greater responsibility to support those efforts more liberally for effective "healing."

> *Congregations need to support and work through public and other specialized church agencies more.*

And I would suggest to you that, as citizens, we also have great responsibility to work always for the kinds of systemic reforms, in our economic and social life, that are the only lasting hope for real social healing and justice in our modern world.

At any rate it is still the three miracles that are needed, for the good of ourselves and of others:

- the miracle of stopping, to examine our paths and affirm our values,
- the miracle of asking, to learn what the greatest needs really are,
- the miracle of healing, which is made possible by the sharing of God's amazing grace when stopping and asking have gone before.

Amen.

> *And the unclean spirit, convulsing him and crying with a loud voice, came out of him.*
> *(Mark 1:26)*

Inner Peace: A Communion Meditation

Mark 1:21-28

T his scripture passage relates the very first story in the Gospel of Mark that talks about the public ministry of Jesus. Of the various stories he could have started with, Mark chose this one.

It is about bringing inner peace to a troubled person, or as said in the ancient world, a person *possessed* by an unclean or evil spirit.

The setting of the story is a synagogue, on the sabbath.

> *There is no escape from life's tragedies.*
> *Attending church every Sunday will not protect us from attempts by the world's evil spirits to "possess" us.*

This reminds us that there is no escape from life's tragedies. Attending church every Sunday will not protect you or me from attempts by the world's evil spirits to *possess* us.

Cancer will invade the bodies of some of us, both outside and inside the *sanctuary* walls.

The long tentacles of war's tragedy will creep even into this room, thousands of miles away from bloody battlefields.

The demons of personal fears and insecurities are indiscriminate about the addresses they choose. Even Paul confessed, "I do not understand my own actions. For I do not do what I want, but I do the very thing I hate" (Rom. 7:15).

> *The demons of personal fears and insecurities are indiscriminate about the addresses they choose.*

Half the truth of this little story is that it takes place in the synagogue on the sabbath. The other half is that belief in Christ can bring inner peace to a troubled soul that has been possessed.

Note that there are no exhortations in this story. No commandments. No "thou shalt nots." Not even any directives or challenges for the future. What is included is the presence of Christ: the acceptance of Christ's kind of love, of Christ's kind of confidence, both of which are apparent.

What is Christ's kind of love, that can conquer evil spirits?

- It is a love that values most highly, not things, but God's Spirit. "For what will it profit them to gain the whole world and forfeit their life?" (Mark 8:36)
- It is a love that seeks not one's own advancement, but the advancement of others. "How happy are those who know their need for God, for the kingdom of Heaven is theirs!"
  (Matt. 5:3, Phillips)
- It is a love that does not condemn others, but helps them. "Blessed are the merciful, for they will receive mercy."
  (Matt. 5:7)
- It is a love that does not exclude, but includes. "Let anyone among you who is without sin be the first to throw a stone at her." (John 8:7)

In the metaphor of this ancient miracle story, the incorporation of Christ's kind of love into our inner beings is part of the power that drives out the evil spirits.

> *The incorporation of Christ's kind of love into our inner beings is part of the power that drives out the evil spirits.*

The other part is Christ's kind of confidence. And make no mistake. Great confidence is necessary if our possession by evil spirits is to end. For they don't want to leave. They live on our doubts and fears.

In the story, when the presence of Christ entered the one *possessed,* "The unclean spirit, convulsing him and crying with a loud voice, came out of him."

Other translations make the evil spirit's protest even stronger: "At this the evil spirit convulsed the man, let out a loud scream and left him!" (Phillips)

It takes Christ's kind of confidence. And what is that?

- It is a confidence that the values of God in life will be sustained though the earth should change. The psalmist expressed it:

God is our refuge and strength,
  a very present help in trouble.
Therefore we will not fear, though the earth should change,
  though the mountains shake in the heart of the sea;
though its waters roar and foam,
  though the mountains tremble with its tumult. . . .
[For then we will remember]
"Be still, and know that I am God!" (Ps. 46:1-3, 10)

- It is a confidence that resisting the evil spirits of the world will ultimately be worthwhile.

Those who conquer will inherit these things, and I will be their God and they will be my children. (Rev. 21:7)

The word *confidence* is from the Latin *confidero;* literally "with trust." To live with Christ's confidence is to live with the trust that

33

God will never forsake, regardless of how much the evil spirits seem, for the moment, to be in control.

It is the theme of James Russell Lowell's great poem "The Present Crisis," from which come the words of our stirring hymn:

> Though the cause of Evil prosper, yet 'tis Truth alone is strong, . . .
> Though her portion be the scaffold, And upon the throne be wrong:
> Yet that scaffold sways the future, and, behind the dim unknown
> Standeth God within the shadow, Keeping watch above his own.

On the cross, Christ himself cried out, "My God, my God, why have you forsaken me?" (Matt. 27:46). But his final words were not of fear, but of the confidence of inner peace: "Father, into your hands I commend my spirit" (Luke 23:46).

On this sabbath we share the sacrament of Holy Communion, initiated by Christ. In this "synagogue," on this sabbath, Christ offers yet to displace the evil spirits of hate and fear, and replace them with his presence of love and confidence.

It is not insignificant, I would suggest to you, that the nutritious-ness of grain is realized only when it is ground for bread. The sweet taste of the grape is released only when it is crushed for drink.

When the evil spirits of the world seem grinding and crushing, then may especially be the time to invite the Spirit of Christ to enter your life with his inner peace. Amen.

> *When Jesus saw him lying there and knew that he had been there a long time, he said to him, "Do you want to be made well?" John 5:6*

Do You Really Want to Be Healed?

John 5:1-9

*T*hat Bethzatha pool referred to in the scripture reading has been excavated in Jerusalem. It is trapezoidal in shape; up to 500 feet wide and 315 long—considerably larger than a football field. A lot of sick people could gather around it.

It was divided through the middle by a partition. On the partition, and also along the sides, were porticoes. It was under the porticoes that the sick lay in the shade. At each corner there were steps that led down into the water.

Jerusalem was a hilly city. The water came from both underground drainage and intermittent springs. Sometimes the water would bubble up from an unseen force. Tradition said that it was an angel stirring the water, and whoever entered it first would be healed. Some ancient manuscripts add to the scripture: "For an angel of the Lord went down at certain seasons into the pool, and stirred up the water; whoever stepped in first after the stirring of the water was made well."

The subject of this miracle story is a man who has been ill for thirty-eight years and still keeps coming to the pool, presumably trying to be the first one in after the water is stirred. Now it doesn't really say that he has come every day for thirty-eight years. But he might have. And if he had done so every day for thirty-eight years, that means that he would have come nearly fourteen thousand times! Still, he is a failure! Someone always beats him into the water! For thirty-eight years! For thousands of days! "Sir, I have no one to put me into the pool when the water is stirred up; and while I am making my way, someone else steps down ahead of me." If you want a biblical example of "hanging in there," this is surely it. Thirty-eight years!

And yet, there seems to be something else to this story, doesn't there? something besides the apparent? a strange twist? a mystery? And that is suggested by Jesus' question to him. For Jesus does not immediately congratulate him for this apparently faithful persistence. Rather, he asks him a question: "Do you want to be made well?"

A strange question to someone who has been coming for thirty-eight years. Still Jesus asks it. "Do you really want to be healed?" Other translations have it: "Do you want to get well again?" (Phillips). "Would you like to get well?" (TLB). "Do you want to recover?" (NEB).

I would guess that every reader has known someone with alcoholism. It is well known that nothing can really happen to control that disease until enough desire for change is truly there. A person must decide, "Yes, I honestly want to recover!" Otherwise, all the pious talk, all the intermittent efforts, all the begging for sympathy, can amount to worse than nothing, both for the alcoholic and for those trying to help—especially when stretched over thirty-eight years!

"Do you really want to be made well?" When I try to interpolate what isn't said in this story, I sometimes think that maybe this man, throughout the thirty-eight years, really has not wanted to get well at all. Perhaps that is why he is never first in the pool.

> *Maybe this man has not wanted to get well at all. Perhaps that is why he is never first in the pool.*

"Why?" you ask. "Why wouldn't he want to be healed?"

Let me suggest three possible reasons that I see acted out in human behavior yet today.

The first is *perfectionism.*

Maybe this man is a perfectionist who, having received a setback, is now afraid even to try because he knows he will probably not be as quick as others. He is not about to set himself up for an embarrassing failure. So he won't do anything. "If you can't do it well, don't do it at all," was drummed into him as a child. Now, believing he should be able to dance down the stairs, he would rather lie helpless than reveal his limping walk.

An early Charles Schulz cartoon has Charlie Brown and Linus leaning on a wall, watching the sunset:

"I hate to see the sun go down," says Charlie. "I've wasted another day."

Linus asks, "What do you consider a day not wasted?"

Charlie responds, "A day where I met the girl of my dreams, was elected President of our country, won a Nobel prize, and hit a home run!"

To which Linus concludes, "I can understand why you hate to see the sun go down."

Where would some of the great heroes of the faith have been if they had waited for perfection before they moved—if they had been afraid even to try?

Moses said, "O my Lord, I have never been eloquent, . . . I am slow of speech and slow of tongue" (Exod. 4:10). Paul wrote of the "thorn" in his flesh (2 Cor. 12:7). Peter wept because he had been such a coward. Yet, they were willing to do what they could with what they had. And perhaps it was even because of their woundedness, their humanity, that they were so effective. Ofttimes life's bad breaks do make people more understanding, both of others and of God. Ambrose Bierce, in *The Devil's Dictionary,* defined a saint as "a dead sinner revised and edited."

Jesus needs to know whether this man really wants to be made well, or whether he is afraid even to try because he might not completely succeed.

Second, maybe he doesn't want to be made well because he is a *slave to the past.*

Perhaps he is so hooked to what has been, that he has stopped looking ahead to what might be. Perhaps he really has become quite comfortable blaming his troubles on the bad fortune of the past, and everyone else: "I have no one to put me into the pool." Perhaps he is scared to break old relationships, even though they are dependent and destructive, and to face the prospect of standing on his own two feet. Perhaps "Pity poor me," rather than "Now here's my plan," has become his motto.

> *Perhaps he is so hooked on what has been, that he has stopped looking ahead to what might be.*

Psychologist Sam Keen, in his book *Beginnings Without End,* says, "The future begins when I cease to rehearse old scenes in which I recite lines written for me by the directors. When I become my own playwright I act in a drama I helped to create. The play begins when I become the author, the authority, of my own life."

Third, maybe this man, after thirty-eight years, is suffering from a *loss of hope.*

Viktor Frankl, a Jewish psychotherapist who survived the Auschwitz death camp, wrote about it in his little classic, *Man's Search for Meaning.* He reports:

> The death rate in the week between Christmas, 1944, and New Year's, 1945, increased in camp beyond all previous experience. . . . The explanation for this increase did not lie in the harder working conditions or the deterioration of our food supplies or a change of weather or new epidemics. It was simply that the majority of the prisoners had lived in the naive hope that they would be home again by Christmas. As the time drew near and there was no encouraging news, the prisoners lost courage and disappointment overcame them.

Losing spiritual hope, they let themselves physically die.

Nietzsche said, "He who has a *why* to live for can bear with almost any *how.*"

Frankl's philosophy, called logotherapy, might be expressed, "A person can bear almost any amount of suffering, so long as that for which one suffers has adequate ultimate meaning."

Well, maybe—maybe these are some of the reasons Jesus asked the question, "Do you want to be made well?"

Are you afraid to try because you might not be perfect?

Are you so rehearsing the past and your disappointment in others that you cannot declare your own future?

Are you a person without hope, who has surrendered prematurely?

At any rate, in the biblical narrative, this miracle story—like all the others—has a happy ending. Apparently Jesus is pleased with the answer he perceives, so he says in effect:

Bless you, my friend. You have been dragging yourself here all this time. Such hope! Such desire to improve as much as you can! Such willingness to seek help, even with the odds of thirty-eight years and the thoughtlessness of others against you! You have hung in there; you have kept the faith. You do want to be made well. So I say to you, stand up, take up your mat, and walk.

The question the story puts to us yet today is this: Knowing our own physical, mental, spiritual, and social illnesses, do we really want to be made well? "Yes" to that question is the beginning if there are to be any more miracles happening in our lives and our world. Amen.

Miracles Beyond Nature

> *Joseph, son of David, do not be afraid to take Mary as your wife, for the child conceived in her is from the Holy Spirit. Matt. 1:20*

Joseph's Trust

Matthew 1:18-25

You can hardly blame Joseph for deciding to divorce Mary when he finds out that she is pregnant, through no fault of his.

Matthew describes Mary and Joseph as being "engaged." But engagement was a much more binding condition then than it is today. It was tantamount to marriage itself, without sexual consummation. Therefore the euphemistic "before they lived together, she was found to be with child." During the chaste engagement period, which usually lasted a year, a man and a woman nevertheless were legally husband and wife. The engagement could be broken only by divorce. If the man died, the woman was considered a widow.

Therefore, Joseph has a big problem. He loves Mary and partly wants to believe her. However, her story of being visited by the angel Gabriel, and being told that God is going to work through her in some fantastic ways, is hard to believe. But so are a lot of other things.

What will people think? He can hear the guys at the carpentry shop now:

> Hey, I hear Mary's pregnant already?
> By the Holy Spirit, you say. Yeah, man.

Joseph's first decision is to divorce her. That will be the easy way out. He will do it quietly, proving he is a caring man ("being a righteous man and unwilling to expose her to public disgrace"). But he will do it nevertheless, proving he is nobody's fool.

> *Joseph's first decision is to divorce her. He will do it quietly, proving he is a caring man, and that he's nobody's fool.*

Something haunts him about his decision though. Rather than filled with peace of mind, he finds himself agonizing more. "It's not consistent . . . Mary's never lied to me before . . . What if it's true?"

It's one of those judgment calls that wakes you at two-thirty in the morning in a cold sweat. You know that a great deal hangs on your decision. You so want it to be right. You pray for help.

And, as the story goes, Joseph's prayer is answered in a dream. Dreams, I believe, are often important conveyors to us of messages about our spiritual lives. Joseph's dream is that Mary is telling the truth. God is going to intercede directly in human life through her, and Joseph also is needed.

Don't be afraid, Joseph. Take a chance.
If it works, the whole world will be changed.

And so Joseph changes his mind and decides to trust. His trust is that God does care enough about people to enter personally the human situation. And that is what is about to happen in Joseph's life, extraordinarily!

> *Joseph changes his mind and decides to trust. He trusts that God does care enough about people to personally enter the human situation.*

His decision is whether to go with his dream or with public opinion; his faith or his fear; the angel of his hopes or the devil of his doubts.

It is a risk of trust someone needs to take. Six centuries before, Isaiah had proclaimed, "Therefore the Lord himself will give you a sign. Look, the young woman is with child and shall bear a son, and shall name him Immanuel" (Isa. 7:14).

Maybe he is needed to help make the dream come true. Now wouldn't that be something!

On the face of it, of course, it is an outrageous idea. Who ever heard of God getting involved in human misery? Presidents don't stand in food lines. Generals don't die in trenches.

The famous German film director Rainer Werner Fassbinder was walking down a New York City street. Noted also for his enormous ego, he usually ignored people who did not work for him. But a young admirer passed him and thought he recognized him. Coming back, and circling around him, the admirer finally said, "You know, you look like the famous German movie director, Rainer Werner Fassbinder." To which Fassbinder replied, "No, he's much too famous. He would never walk down this street."

Friends, the primary premise of the Christian faith is that God walks down these streets.

No stable is too lowly.
No family is too poor.
No situation is too hopeless.
Even through the valley of the shadow of death, God walks with us.
Even through divorce, and other intersections that require agonizing decisions,
the same God of creation walks with us down these streets.

The coming of God to you—your Emmanuel—may not be through angelburst and stardust. It is unlikely that even poor shepherds will notice your visitation, let alone magi from the east. But isn't that the beauty of it? The premise is that God's coming is tailored to us: to our places, to our time, to our needs. And so quietly: as if a seed were being carefully planted in well-prepared soil, to begin gently growing.

> *The premise is that God's coming is tailored to us:*
> *to our places, time, and needs.*

Phillips Brooks put it:

> How silently, how silently, the wondrous gift is given;
> so God imparts to human hearts the blessings of his heaven.
> No ear may hear his coming, but in this world of sin,
> where meek souls will receive him, still the dear Christ enters in.

Really believing that, Joseph decides to act in trust. By the way, after this initial episode, Joseph apparently learns to trust much more in his own inner voice, his instincts, his feelings, his dreams, his angel. In modern parlance, he listens to the impulses of his right brain as well as to the logic of his left brain. In making important decisions, he learns not only to read the opinion polls of other people, but also to broaden his own prayer life.

In the second chapter of Matthew, Joseph has three more dreams that are pivotal for the holy family. The first warns them to escape Herod's paranoia by fleeing to Egypt. The second sends them back to Israel after Herod dies. The third directs them to Nazareth, where Jesus is to grow up known as the carpenter Joseph's son.

Another important element in Joseph's willingness to trust is his courage to take a risk.

Gail Sheehy, in her helpful book *Pathfinders,* writes:

> One of the first things I discovered about pathfinders is that they are willing to risk change. They do not expect to cruise through life in a sports car along a well-marked superhighway. Confronted with an obstacle or an accident along the way, they try a detour that usually turns out to be constructive. . . . A willingness to risk is the master quality for pathfinding.

Well, that turns out to be Joseph. If you can't afford a camel, then get a good donkey. But go! If you can't get into the inn, then move out to the stable. But move!

> *If you can't afford a camel, then get a good donkey. But go! If you can't get into the inn, then move out to the stable. But move!*

I remember a Christmas in the bleak Depression of the 1930s when my father cut a hole in our kitchen wall.

For many months he had saved money from his meager earnings to buy my mother her first electric refrigerator. It was delivered on Christmas Eve. The only trouble was that it wouldn't fit in the kitchen of our tiny house. "Bill, what have you done?" exclaimed my mother. "That won't fit in here!" "Oh yes it will," replied my dad. "I'm going to cut a hole in the wall. Its back will stick into our bedroom, but it will be worth it!"

Work started yet that night, and by Christmas night the job was done. Though we lived in the smallest house on the block, we had an electric refrigerator in our kitchen! My dad decided not to wait until we could afford a bigger house. He cut through a wall of the house where we were. For him, progress had already been delayed too long.

And years later my father's bold act, born out of his love for my mother, became a metaphor for me of Joseph's courage to risk, born of his trust in God.

Which risks to take have to be chosen prayerfully by all the Josephs and Marys of the world, listening equally to the realities of the commitments they have made, and to the dreams of what they might yet be called to dare.

The original Joseph, the New Testament testifies, was right in his trust. The doctrine of the Virgin Birth was the early Christians' way of saying:

Yes. God does intervene in human affairs in strange and mysterious ways. Jesus was not the pinnacle of human evolution, but the intervention of a transcendent God into human history. It means that the Creator God used earthbound flesh, blood, and mind to communicate with the world on its own terms.

47

And Christians ever since, regardless of their dogma differences, have been united in seeing Jesus as the fulfillment of the promise made to Joseph:

> Joseph, son of David, do not be afraid to take Mary as your wife, for the child conceived in her is from the Holy Spirit. She will bear a son, and you are to name him Jesus, for he will save his people from their sins.

The word *Jesus* means "God saves." Jesus Emmanuel means "God is with us to save." Joseph, by his prayerful trust in a miraculous possibility, was saved from a dreadful mistake.

May you and I learn from Joseph's prayerful trust in making our own decisions. Amen.

> *When the steward tasted the water that had become wine, and did not know where it came from . . ., the steward called the bridegroom and said to him, "Everyone serves the good wine first, and then the inferior wine after the guests have become drunk. But you have kept the good wine until now."*
> *John 2:9-10*

Filling Empty Jars

John 2:1-11

Joseph Campbell, in his excellent interviews with Bill Moyers about myths, said, "Myths are stories of our search through the ages for truth, for meaning, for significance."

Myths deal with more than history. Myths, from every age and every people, deal with realities beyond the known facts, beneath and above the present consciousness. Said Campbell, "It is out of the depths of the unconscious that the energies of life come to us. . . . This cauldron is the inexhaustible source, the center, the bubbling spring from which life proceeds."

Robert Fulghum, in his popular book *All I Really Need to Know I Learned in Kindergarten*, makes the same point. The "Storyteller's Creed," he says, begins:

> I believe that imagination is stronger than knowledge.
> That myth is more potent than history.
> That dreams are more powerful than facts.

The purpose of these sermons on the miracles of Jesus is not to argue their physical details. It is rather to search out what might be their hidden, even unconscious, spiritual meanings—both for those who first told and then wrote them, and for us centuries later. In other words, are there basic yearnings and learnings that all people have in common, wherever and whenever they live?

According to the Gospel of John, the first miracle of Jesus took place at a wedding in the village of Cana, about nine miles north of Nazareth, Jesus' hometown.

First some background.

A wedding in those days was no thirty-minute affair followed by an afternoon or evening reception. In an observant Jewish family, the wedding included a feast that continued for several days, with fresh guests arriving each day.

Jesus, along with other members of his family, has been invited to this wedding. But because he has been down south with John the Baptist, and then busy calling his first disciples, he arrives late, bringing his disciples with him. It is not surprising then, that when he and his disciples get there on perhaps the fifth or sixth day, he finds that the supply of wine is exhausted. The jars are empty!

Let me say something also about wine in the Jewish tradition. The prophet Amos, in the last chapter of his book, where he shares his vision of the good life, says:

> The mountains shall drip sweet wine,
> and all the hills shall flow with it. (9:13)

In another Jewish writing of almost the same time as the Gospel of John, there is this description of the fantastic abundance which is to come when God's way rules:

> The earth shall yield its fruit ten thousandfold; each vine shall have 1000 branches; each branch 1000 clusters; each cluster 1000 grapes; and each grape about 120 gallons of wine. (2 Bar. xxix.5)

How would you like to own that vineyard?

Well then, for a marriage to start with the symbol of empty wine jars would be a bad omen indeed, with little chance of ever achieving its potential.

> *For a marriage to start with the symbol of empty wine jars would be a bad omen, indeed, with little chance of ever achieving its full potential.*

And so the miracle is described. Six clay jars stand nearby. That was the number required for the water used in the purification rites in an observant Jewish home. Each jar can hold twenty to thirty gallons—the size of a large garbage can. Jesus asks the servants to fill the empty jars with water from the well. That means, when they are done, 120 to 180 gallons! He then instructs them to draw some and take it, as one translation says, "to the headwaiter" (NASB). That experienced connoisseur, on tasting it, discovers that it is not only more wine, but very fine wine, of extraordinary quality. Thinking that the bridegroom has finally opened some secret supply of his own, he exclaims to him: "Everybody I know puts his good wine on first and then when [people] have had plenty to drink, he brings out the poor stuff. But you have kept back your good wine till now!" (2:10 Phillips).

And the story concludes: "Jesus did this, the first of his signs, in Cana of Galilee, and revealed his glory; and his disciples believed in him."

To say the least, it is an unusual biblical story, for several reasons. First, it is told only in the Gospel of John. Matthew, Mark, and Luke, all written earlier, ignore it altogether.

Second, there is this curious put-down of Mary, his mother, when she tries to tell him what he ought to do. "Woman, what concern is that to you and to me? My hour has not yet come." In other words, "Back off, Mom, Don't push me!" All Mary can do is whisper to puzzled servants who have witnessed this family flare-up, "Do whatever he tells you."

Third, Jesus has the poor servants draw all that water from the well unnecessarily, doesn't he? I mean if he can perform the miracle of making wine, why not just do it? What's this business of needing water first? He should think about the servants' aching backs as well as the guests' appetites.

Fourth, to be honest, it is not a miracle of really great consequence. So some people have to do without wine. They'll probably just go earlier to the next wedding! Certainly it is not in a league with the healing of blind Bartimaeus or the raising of Lazarus from the dead.

And fifth, it is a miracle that has its definite downside. I don't have to tell you who are or know victims of alcoholism, that too much wine can also be very bad news. We don't know anything about the bridegroom or the guests. Knowing himself and them, did he intend to be cautious about how much wine was made available?

But, to get hung up on those questions would be, remembering the "Storyteller's Creed," to treat the story only as "knowledge, . . . history, . . . facts" and miss the "imagination, . . . myth, . . . dreams," which are in their messages for us, even "stronger, . . . more potent, . . . more powerful."

For instance, here are some of the things the story says to me. When the jars of our lives are empty; when we are exhausted, drained, emptied by the unexpected demands put upon us by life's sometimes unpredictable circumstances, then:

First, keep believing in self. However empty our jars and whatever our circumstances, our worth is just as great and our need is just as recognized by God as was that of that unknown bride and groom in Cana, whose story was told only by John.

> *When the jars of our lives are empty; when we are exhausted, drained, and emptied by the unexpected demands of life's sometimes unpredictable circumstances, then this miracle story teaches us.*

Second, accept personal responsibility. Just as Jesus had to declare independence from his advice-giving mother, so we have to reach a point where not the opinions of others, but our own values and instincts guide us.

Third, get to work. That's the meaning to me of the servants having to draw the water before Jesus will make the wine. Human effort and divine grace meet. Both are essential to the other if the miracle is to succeed.

Fourth, take some risks. Everything may not turn out wonderful. Too much wine may have been a problem for some in Cana. But those who make no mistakes in their lives are also those whose jars are never brimful and whose cups never "runneth over."

> *Those who make no mistakes in their lives are also those whose jars are never brimful, and whose cups never "runneth over."*

Fifth, hang in there. Patient constancy now may result in future blessings that far exceed your expectations. John says of this strange little story in a tiny village, unreported by anyone else, "This, the first of his signs . . . revealed his glory; and his disciples believed in him."

Finally, is there any message in this miracle story for today's church? One congregation applied its teachings directly to the need for decent and affordable low-cost housing in their city. They renovated an abandoned brick four-plex to provide attractive apartments for four families. They even called the project "Miracle on 12th Street."

How did the old miracle story inform this church in the present? First, to succeed, its members had to believe that an abandoned, empty building on 12th Street was just as important as those drained, empty jars in Cana. In fact, they came to believe that a great deal of progress was being made to fill, not empty jars with wine, but an empty building with families.

Second, they had to accept some personal responsibility for helping to house the poor of their city and to reclaim a declining neighborhood—as Jesus, with or without his mother's urging, took responsibility for helping "save" the wedding feast. Opinions, study, advice could have gone on forever. There came a time for decision, commitment, and action.

Third, they had to go to work through their money and volunteer labor, what they called "sweat equity." No work by them—no miracle by God, this story says. If the servants (that's today's Christians) don't draw the water (that's money and effort) then the empty jars won't be filled with new wine (or apartments filled with needy families).

Fourth, they had to take a risk. Just as Jesus couldn't know the whole effect of all that wedding wine, the church members couldn't know the results of all their efforts and gifts. Still, their Christian conscience called them to act. Elie Wiesel, Nobel Prize–winning survivor of Hitler's death camps, being asked why he continued to cry out about human violence and evil, when the world seems to get no better, replied, "It is for myself. It is to live with myself."

Fifth, they had to believe that God could make of their miracle also a "sign" that would "reveal Christ's glory" and lead others to "believe in him." When Jesus announced his public ministry at his home synagogue in Nazareth, he began,

> The Spirit of the Lord is upon me,
>   because he has anointed me
>   to bring good news to the poor. (Luke 4:18)

The miracle of filling the empty jars said to that congregation that the best way to preach is to do, and the best way to get people to follow Jesus' way is to meet human need.

Are the miracles dead stories of ancient history? I suggest to you that they are alive with meanings that can change history—yours and mine, private and public.

And I pray that that may be the power of our faith. Amen.

The Boat Is Sinking

> *He woke up and rebuked the wind, and said to
> the sea, "Peace! Be still!" Then the wind ceased,
> and there was a dead calm.*
> *Mark 4:39*

Keeping Still
in the Storm

Mark 4:35-41

*T*his is one of my favorite miracle stories. I love its
robust drama, counterbalanced with a light touch of
humor. I love its message, both for the early Christians, entering the period of persecutions, and for us,
whatever the stormy seas we have to cross.

With an economy of words, the drama is barely outlined. It is
evening. The sun has set. The day is done. The disciples are tired.
For several days there have been huge crowds beside the Sea of
Galilee, pressing in, wanting to discuss Jesus' teachings. This day
they had put him off shore in a boat so he could be seen and heard
by more. Who knows what will happen tomorrow? Maybe the revo-
lution will start here, and Jesus will be its general. The disciples are
both excited by the signs of success in the thousands of people
assembled and sobered by the responsibilities that may fall on them.

And then their evening reverie is broken by those simple words,
"Let us go across to the other side."

"You've gotta be kidding!" "He must be crazy!" "It's madness to leave all this just when we're on the brink of success." "The other side? Who cares about the other side? They're not our kind. Everybody knows the Gerasenes over there are just a bunch of pagans. We've got more than we can handle taking care of ourselves, let alone worrying about them."

"The other side? Who cares about the other side? They're not our kind. We've got more than we can handle taking care of ourselves."

"Well I don't know about all that. But I'm sure not anxious to try a five-mile crossing, at night, with the smell of a storm in the air, to anywhere!"

Nevertheless, they are soon on their way, with their fears increasing even further as the land disappears from sight.

And then the storm hits. Swooping down in the darkness from the eastern mountains, the winds whip the sea into a frenzy. Waves grow larger and larger. The boat is going out of control, swamped with frothing water as wave after wave crashes over it.

"Didn't I tell you! Didn't I tell you! This whole idea is crazy! Why couldn't he leave well enough alone? It's going to be the end of us all. . . . By the way, where is he?"

Good question! Where is Jesus? What is he doing to help save them all from perishing on this ill-fated crossing? Is he as frightened as they are, as they behave like a flock of Chicken Littles cackling, "The sky is falling! The sky is falling!"?

And then they find him. Incredible! Astonishing! He will never cease to amaze them! With the waves crashing, and the wind howling, and the thunder rumbling, and the lightning making it momentarily as bright as day, they find Jesus, on a cushion, in the stern, sound asleep.

Now that's cool!

> *With the waves crashing, the wind howling,*
> *the thunder rumbling, and the lightning*
> *making it momentarily as bright as day, they find*
> *Jesus, on a cushion, in the stern, sound asleep.*

But their first reaction is anger. "Teacher, do you not care that we are perishing?"

And then comes this miracle. Jesus "awoke and rebuked the wind, and said to the sea, 'Peace! Be still!' " (RSV). The New Jerusalem Bible has it, "Quiet now! Be calm!"

The wind ceases and there is "a dead calm." And then Jesus says to the disciples, "Why are you afraid? Have you still no faith?"

What comfort and encouragement this story must have been for the early Christians as they moved out on their frightening crossings:

- as they crossed over from slavery to freedom
- as they crossed over from subservience to self-confidence
- as they crossed over from class discrimination to dignity
- as they crossed over from unthinking habits to new discoveries
- as they crossed over from denial of reality to confrontation with it
- as they crossed over from obeying the emperor to serving humanity
- as they crossed over from Caesar to Christ.

For their crossings, too, were on hostile seas. The values they proclaimed challenged old authorities and threatened the world's order. Resistance was inevitable. They were charged by old religious rulers with being fanatical heretics. They were charged by entrenched political rulers with being radical subversives.

They were ostracized, outlawed, persecuted, driven underground, martyred. Still, Paul, who was later to be martyred himself, could write to the Christians in Rome, where the storms were the worst:

Who will separate us from the love of Christ? Will hardship, or distress, or persecution, or famine, or nakedness, or peril, or sword? . . . No, in all these things we are more than conquerors through him who loved us. For I am convinced that neither death, nor life, nor angels, nor rulers, nor things present, nor things to come, nor powers, nor height, nor depth, nor anything else in all creation, will be able to separate us from the love of God in Christ Jesus our Lord. (Rom. 8:35, 37-39)

And my hope is that the old story still brings comfort and encouragement yet today to you for the crossings you have to make in your life:

- when you have to cross from what has been to what is yet to become
- when you have to cross from old lands that are familiar to new lands of mystery
- when you have to cross from former successes (or failures) to unforeseen challenges.

The crossings may be precipitated by many things:

- by personal growth through what Gail Sheehy calls the normal "Passages" of human development
- by changes in relationships with others, in or out of marriage
- by career interruption or redirection
- by the bad fortune of failing health or accident
- by the death of a loved one.

Whatever the cause, the miracle of Christ stilling the storm says two things to me. First, rough seas have to be crossed if new lands are to be won.

Second, keep faith that with God's help, you can make it to the other side.

To put it another way: Don't fear the crossing's storm, for Christ is in your boat with you, needing only to be awakened to your need to bring peace and calm.

> *Don't fear the crossing's storm, for Christ is in your boat with you, needing only to be awakened to your need to bring peace and calm.*

What it means is having a basic spiritual faith in the gracious care of God for you, whatever your condition or situation. It is that same ancient faith expressed by a psalmist long before Jesus, but using in poetic form the same imagery:

> Some went down to the sea in ships,
>   doing business on the mighty waters;
> they saw the deeds of the LORD,
>   his wondrous works in the deep.
> For he commanded and raised the stormy wind,
>   which lifted up the waves of the sea.
> They mounted up to heaven, they went down to the depths;
>   their courage melted away in their calamity;
> they reeled and staggered like drunkards,
>   and were at their wits' end.
> Then they cried to the LORD in their trouble,
>   and he brought them out from their distress;
> he made the storm be still,
>   and the waves of the sea were hushed.
> Then they were glad because they had quiet,
>   and he brought them to their desired haven.
> Let them thank the LORD for his steadfast love,
>   for his wonderful works to humankind.
>
>   (Ps. 107:23-31)

It is the faith expressed long after Jesus by Katharina von Schlegel:

> Be still, my soul: your God will undertake
> to guide the future, as in ages past.
> Your hope, your confidence let nothing shake;
> all now mysterious shall be bright at last.
> Be still, my soul: the waves and winds still know
> the Christ who ruled them while he dwelt below.

It is the miracle of keeping still in the soul during the frenzy of life's stormy crossings. May it be a miracle that continues for you. Amen.

> *When it was evening, the disciples came to him and said, "This is a deserted place, and the hour is now late; send the crowds away so that they may go into the villages and buy food for themselves." Jesus said to them, "They need not go away; you give them something to eat."*
> *Matt. 14:15-16*

Ingredients of True Care

Matthew 14:13-21

The feeding of the five thousand is the only miracle story to appear in all four Gospels. As a matter of fact, Matthew and Mark like it so much that they repeat it in slightly different form. And what that shows is the importance that helping others carried in the early Church. It is completely in accord with the combination of religion and ethics portrayed in the First Letter of John:

> Beloved, let us love one another, because love is from God. . . . Those who say, "I love God," and hate their brothers or sisters, are liars; for those who do not love a brother or sister whom they have seen, cannot love God whom they have not seen. The commandment we have from [Christ] is this: those who love God must love their brothers and sisters also. (4:7, 20-21)

For me, this miracle of the feeding teaches three ingredients of true care. The first is a basic feeling of *compassion for others*. Note the context of the story.

Even though opposition to religious reform has begun among the ruling powers, and that is symbolized by the beheading of John the Baptist, Jesus has become extremely popular among the people. The disciples are exhausted by the constant move from town to town. Mark says they had "no leisure even to eat." Finally, to escape, Jesus loads them all on a boat for some solitude and respite out on Galilee. But when they land, an even larger crowd awaits.

The reaction of the disciples is understandable. They are still physically tired and emotionally drained. They say, "This is a deserted place, and the hour is now late; send the crowds away so that they may go into the villages and buy food for themselves."

Jesus' reaction is different. He says, "They need not go away; you give them something to eat."

A very interesting article, "The Heartless Lovers of Humankind," written by historian Paul Johnson, was published in the *Wall Street Journal*. Its thesis was that some of history's greatest minds have done great damage by loving the theoretical idea of humanity, but not the actual individuals who compose it.

> Loving humanity as an idea, they can then produce solutions as ideas. Therein lies the danger, for when people conflict with the solution-as-idea, they are first ignored or dismissed as unrepresentative; and then, when they continue to obstruct the idea, they are treated with growing hostility and categorized as enemies of humanity-in-general.

One of the examples Johnson gives is Karl Marx:

> There was an enormous gap between Marx's egalitarian ideas and the way he actually behaved. . . . He inherited considerable sums of money. He never had less than two servants. He had a horror of what he called "a purely proletarian set-up." He made his wife send out visiting cards in which she was described as "nee Baronesse Westphalen." He would not let his daughters train for any profession or learn anything except to play the piano. . . . He seduced his wife's servant, begot a son by her, then forced Friedrich Engels to assume paternity. . . . He never made a visit to an actual factory.

Contrast that with the basic Christian belief that God so wanted to identify with common people that human flesh was assumed in Jesus. "In the beginning was the Word, and the Word was with God, and the Word was God. . . . And the Word became flesh and lived among us" (John 1:1, 14).

And one can but wonder whether the social, economic, and moral collapse of the ideologically imposed communist systems around the world was not in part because of their institutionalized violations of the basic need of people—real people—both to give and to receive compassion freely, with the help rather than the suppression of their government.

To have Jesus' kind of compassion is truly to respect the value of and to try to meet the needs of real persons.

> *To have Jesus' kind of compassion is truly to respect the value of, and to try to meet the needs of, real persons.*

One of our sons, when in high school, brought home a true story told him by the school custodian. A person charged with trespassing and vandalism at the school was being tried at the county courthouse. Three persons sat in the room outside the court chambers, waiting to be called as witnesses—the principal, the vice principal, and the custodian. The custodian had bought a new suit, he said, for the occasion.

First the bailiff called out, "Send in Mr. Faracci." The principal went in.

Next, a few minutes later, "Send in Mr. Lombardi." The vice principal went in.

Then, "Send in the janitor."

"Now you know," the custodian told John, "why it's sometimes hard to feel that anyone really cares about me around here." Similarly, *Nobody Knows My Name* was the book by James Baldwin that helped launch the modern civil rights movement in this country.

De Chardin brought together human relations and the ideas of religion, ethics, and theology when he said, "The way you treat people is the way you treat God." The story of the feeding of the five thousand begins, "When he went ashore, he saw a great crowd; and he had compassion for them."

The second ingredient of true care that I find in this miracle story is *personal sharing.* "They need not go away; you give them something to eat," says Jesus. The disciples are shocked, incredulous: "We have nothing here but five loaves and two fish." You have to give Jesus this. He never insulted anyone by expecting too little. To the rich young ruler: "Sell all that you own and distribute the money to the poor" (Luke 18:18-30). Zacchaeus ended up giving half his goods to the poor and repaying fourfold those he had cheated (Luke 19:1-10).

Aside from the typical Hebrew hyperbole, one point in this feeding-of-the-five-thousand story is: Never underestimate what your personal deed of compassion may do in the lives of others.

> *Never underestimate what your personal deed of compassion may do in the lives of others.*

How many times has a simple word of sympathy and encouragement by a friend broken one's spell of loneliness and depression? Or a telephone call for no other purpose than to show care? Or a personal note, a dish of tasty food, or cheerful flowers? Such are the loaves and fish that we can share with others, sometimes meager indeed in terms of the needs, but often multiplied in effect, as in the ancient story, far beyond our imaginings.

One of the most helpful social developments in recent years is the hospice movement. Its volunteers show their compassion for the dying, and their families, simply by sitting with patients to provide a respite for family members. These gifts of time and compassionate presence are the loaves and fish that help feed hungry souls with a spiritual food that is priceless.

> *The gifts of time and compassionate presence are the loaves and fish that help feed hungry souls with a spiritual food that is priceless.*

The first ingredient of true care is a basic feeling of compassion for others. The second is personal sharing. And the third is *organized action.*

Compassion without organized action does not provide the training needed by hospice volunteers or a system for their assignment. Compassion without organized action does not deliver Church World Service emergency help to flood, hurricane, and earthquake victims.

And just as the resources of government, community agencies, and churches have to be organized and mobilized to deliver true care where it is needed, so Jesus had to organize that mob beside Galilee.

The story says that the five thousand are divided into groups. Mark specifies groups of fifty and one hundred. Intimacy increases caring.

They are told to sit. Sitting decreases pushing and shoving, and promotes sharing.

But perhaps the main teaching is that, even for Jesus, a huge problem has to be reduced to solvable proportions through prudent management and organization.

> *Even for Jesus, a huge problem had to be reduced to solvable proportions through prudent management and organization.*

One of Charles Schulz's early cartoons has Linus watching TV. His older sister Lucy enters the room and says, "Switch channels! I want to watch MY program!"

"Are you kidding?" asks Linus. "What makes you think you can just walk right in here, and take over?"

Lucy replies, "These five fingers. . . . Individually, they're nothing, but when I curl them together like this into a single unit, they form a weapon that is terrible to behold!"

Linus asks, "Which channel do you want?"

And in the last frame Lucy watches the TV while Linus looks at his five fingers and says, "Why can't you guys get organized like that?"

How the miracle happens we will never know. It starts with the disciples sharing all they have—five loaves and two fish. It ends with "And all ate and were filled; and they took up what was left over of the broken pieces, twelve baskets full."

Novelist Lloyd Douglas suggested that because of the disciples' willingness to share, and Jesus' confidence as expressed in his leadership and blessing, all the people also shared what they had hidden away under their robes in a kind of giant potluck, and there was then much more than enough for all.

Indeed, the biblical story concludes that when everyone showed compassion, there were twelve baskets full of food left over—one for each disciple who had originally doubted.

And that is the biblical promise.

The caring heart that empties itself in compassion for others shall be refilled a dozen times over by the blessings of God's love.

Even the little deeds of caring hearts, by the miracle of God's grace, are multiplied into bushels of love and hope for the whole human race. Amen.

> *But these words seemed to them an idle tale, and they did not believe them.* Luke 24:11

News Too Good to Believe

Luke 24:1-12

*N*onsense!" That was the first reaction to the Easter miracle.

The disciples were tired. They had not slept at all on Friday night. On Saturday they worried all day about their futures. Then the women return from the tomb early Sunday morning, waking them from their first deep sleep in a week, to tell them this incredible tale about Jesus' body being gone.

The New Jerusalem Bible translates the men's response, "pure nonsense, and they did not believe them."

One reason they didn't believe them, of course, was because they were women. Women, in those days, were considered to be of such low estate in public life that they were prohibited from serving as witnesses in court. In matters of religion, their participation in the male-dominated synagogue was forbidden. Now, the male disciples are supposed to believe what the women say they have witnessed at the Lord's tomb? "No way! You've got to be kidding! Do you think we were born yesterday?"

Clarence Jordan, in his "Cotton Patch Version of Luke," paraphrased it, "It all seemed to the men like so much female chatter, and they wouldn't believe it."

Oh, what stones we roll over the openings to one another's lives! "Look, Mom, a butterfly" . . . "Can't you see I'm busy?"

Oh, what creative spirits we imprison in the tombs of our own souls! "After what I've been through, I'm taking no more chances."

Easter says that when you are tired and your perspective is limited, beware that you don't assume the same about that life-giving, always creating Spirit of God within you. Don't limit divine possibilities to the tightness of today's tomb.

> *Easter says that when you are tired and your perspective limited, beware that you don't assume the same about that life-giving, always creating Spirit of God within you.*

One Holy Week I took communion to a nursing home. Not only were there five members of the church I served present, but all Christian residents, including Roman Catholic and Orthodox, were gathered in the lounge for the service. One man kissed my hand when I gave him the elements. I placed my hand on his head and blessed him as his priest. One woman, however, was not so trusting. When I gave her the bread, she asked, "What church are you from?" "The United Church of Christ," I answered. With that, before putting the bread in her mouth, she closed her eyes and said quite firmly, "Presbyterian!" And later, the same with the cup. "Ministering to you in Christ's name, I give you this cup." "Presbyterian!" Gulp.

For this woman's "Presbyterian," substitute:

"Male" (Gulp),	"Female" (Gulp),
"Young" (Gulp),	"Old" (Gulp),
"Poor" (Gulp),	"Rich" (Gulp),
"Liberal" (Gulp),	"Conservative" (Gulp),

and you name some of the other stones we roll over the possible openings for potential human growth and understanding, thereby blocking that indwelling Spirit of God. And when we do, then we too are responding to Easter with, "Nonsense! It's too good to believe!"

Another reason the disciples responded this way to the Good News was that they were in such a negative mood. Fatalistic, you might call it. All day Saturday they had brooded.

In spite of three years of trying, it seemed nothing had changed. Political conniving and violence still won the day. People were just as corruptible and cruel as ever. Even within their ranks, Peter had denied Jesus, and Judas had betrayed him and then committed suicide.

What hope could there possibly be for the kind of changes in people's values that Jesus talked about when even *they* had fallen away? Were Galilean dreams always to be squelched by Jerusalem nightmares? Where did the Palm Sunday supporters disappear to?

As Shakespeare was to have Macbeth summarize life:

> It is a tale
> Told by an idiot, full of sound and fury,
> Signifying nothing.

Yet today, the Easter Good News is still nonsense to those entombed people afraid to open their own lives or let the lives of others be open to the future; to those fatalists who say that the only smart goal is to seek your own security and comfort.

The Easter Good News is still nonsense to those entombed people who are afraid to open their own lives to the future.

Yes, to many, probably the majority, Easter is news too good to believe.

But, to those who can believe Easter's message, as all the disciples—men and women—shortly did, when they discovered the undiminished presence and power of Christ now within themselves—it is yet the source of freedom and hope for self and humankind.

An Easter folk song says:

Christ the Lord is risen from his three-day tomb.
Gone is all our sorrow, gone is all our gloom.

Easter's message does start with the sin and suffering in our lives and in the world. Tomb and gloom. They are real, as was Good Friday. They are not to be denied. Christianity always begins there, in the valley of the shadow, with the pre-Easter cross's reality. Face it, wrestle with it, name it; cry over it, as did Simon Peter.

But then know that your very acknowledgment of that sinful reality, and your creative response to failure and suffering, are the starting points for your new beginnings, your own resurrections.

Paul wrote, "We know that all things work together for good for those who love God, who are called according to his purpose" (Rom. 8:28).

The psalmist prayed, "Out of the depths I cry to you, O LORD! / Lord, hear my voice!" (Ps. 130:1-2).

And Easter is God's supreme response: "I hear you from your depths. I understand. I will help you. For I have been there too."

Easter is beyond our scientific, technological explanations. It is a miracle that cries out for symbols.

The egg. Looking at an egg for the first time, who could possibly imagine its breaking open to reveal a live, fuzzy, perky chick, ready to take on the world?

The lily. Imagine uptight buds opening to trumpet the good news.

The Easter bunny. Yes, the bunny, with its wonderful hop. Did you know, by the way, that the words *hop* and *hope* come from the same root? That's right. You might even say that to live with hope is to keep hopping when everything seems hopeless!

> *The words hop and hope come from the same root. You might say that to live with hope is to keep hopping when everything seems hopeless.*

Consider an Easter Bunny translation of the scriptures. Paul:

For in hop we were saved. (Rom. 8:24)

or

May the God of hop fill you with all joy and peace in believing,
so that you may abound in hop by the power of the Holy Spirit.
(Rom. 15:13)

or

Since, then, we have such a hop, we act with great boldness.
(2 Cor. 3:12)

And Peter:

By his great mercy [God] has given us a new birth into a living
hop through the resurrection of Jesus Christ from the dead.
(1 Pet. 1:3)

Jesus' death on the cross is the symbol of all our deaths: deaths
of our relationships, marriages, jobs, dreams, loved ones, and our
own bodies.

Jesus' resurrection is the symbol of all our resurrections: our
beginnings of new life where we thought none was possible ever
again.

Psychologist Sam Keen says, "Hope is the radical refusal to calcu-
late the limits of the possible."

Poet Thomas Carlisle says:

> Every morning
> can be an Easter
> celebrating
> another happy ending
> and a new beginning
> annunciating
> that God loves us.*

Is Easter nonsense to you, news too good to believe? I pray not.
For it truly is God's most special gift of hope, intended to give life
its sense. May it do so for you. Amen.

---

*Reprinted from *Mistaken Identity* by Thomas John Carlisle, © 1973 by Wm. B. Eerdmans
Publishing Co., used with permission.

Miracles of the Spirit

And his commandments are not burdensome, for whatever is born of God conquers the world.
1 John 5:3-4

"Miracle Lite"

1 John 5:1-5

D o you know why angels can fly?
A wonderful answer was given by that wise British wit, G. K. Chesterton, who said, "Angels can fly because they take themselves lightly."
And that reminds me of another delightful saying by another Briton. Winston Churchill, contemplating the sad state of the human condition, said to his daughter Violet Asquith, "We are all worms, but I do believe I am a glow-worm."

In other words, friends, lighten up! Otherwise, you'll never fly, or glow!

To be Christian is to be freed to glow and fly.

To be Christian is not to be bound to the earth with religious burdens, but to be freed to glow and fly, to be "Miracle Lite" because of our experience of God's love. That's what I hear the writer of the little letter called 1 John saying to the early Church.

73

For the love of God is this, that we obey his commandments. And his commandments are not burdensome, for whatever is born of God conquers the world. (5:3-4)

The First Letter of John was written at about the turn of the first century. It is two generations since Jesus was on earth. All the original disciples have died. Now conflicts have arisen over what it means to be Christian.

Some say it means adherence to particular religious dogmas. Some say it means subjection to certain ecclesiastical authorities. Some say it means the inclusion of certain kinds of people and the exclusion of others.

This little letter says, you're making it too heavy. Lighten up, folks!

The New Jerusalem Bible has it: "This is what the love of God is: keeping his commandments. Nor are his commandments burdensome."

What are God's commandments? First John 3:23 summarizes them this way: "That we should believe in the name of his Son Jesus Christ and love one another." And it goes on to say that we can lighten up and continue being lovers of life and others, even when the world's burdens get heavy, because, in the words of our text, "Whatever is born of God conquers the world."

One of the chief miracles that the early Christians saw in Jesus was his ability to conquer the evil and hatred in the world around him with his overcoming love. Even on the cross he could pray for his enemies and all those who forsook him. "Father, forgive them; for they do not know what they are doing" (Luke 23:34). It was such love that liberated Christ to be "Miracle Lite." And so he could assure the repentant thief, "Truly I tell you, today you will be with me in Paradise" (Luke 23:43), and later make his last words before his resurrection, "Father, into your hands I commend my spirit" (Luke 23:46).

No wonder the religion of Jesus was seen to be not a burden, but a joy. And it was consistent with all his teachings. Among his criticisms of the scribes and Pharisees were, "They tie up heavy burdens, hard to bear, and lay them on the shoulders of others" (Matt. 23:4). As for himself:

Come to me, all you that are weary and are carrying heavy burdens, and I will give you rest. Take my yoke upon you, and learn from me;

for I am gentle and humble in heart, and you will find rest for your souls. For my yoke is easy, and my burden is light. (Matt. 11:28-30)

And what is that yoke of Christ, that burden that is light? He spelled it out for the disciples after the Last Supper: "I give you a new commandment, that you love one another. Just as I have loved you, you also should love one another. By this everyone will know that you are my disciples, if you have love for one another" (John 13:34-35).

Next to the lightening miracle of love, what greater miracle is possible? Indeed, the plea to "lighten up" was not even new with Jesus in the history of our faith. In the book of Deuteronomy, Moses says:

> Surely, this commandment that I am commanding you today is not too hard for you, nor is it too far away. It is not in heaven, that you should say, "Who will go up to heaven for us, and get it for us so that we may hear it and observe it?" Neither is it beyond the sea, that you should say, "Who will cross to the other side of the sea for us, and get it for us so that we may hear it and observe it?" No, the word is very near to you; it is in your mouth and in your heart for you to observe. (30:11-14)

Lighten up, folks! That is what it is all saying. Accept the "heredity" of God's love within you. Let it enable you to fly! Let it make you glow! It is a plea for a philosophy of life.

Lighten up! Accept the "heredity" of God's love within you.

Theologian Karl Rahner speaks of the "grave-merry" person. The grave-merry person is one who lives "with an easy gaiety of spirit, . . . of spiritual elegance," who lives in "invincible security." Such people, he says, see "through the tragically ridiculous masks of the game of life" and have "taken the measure of the cramping boundaries of our earthly existence."

It's like the good wife in the book of Proverbs:

> Strength and dignity are her clothing,
> and she laughs at the time to come. (31:25)

75

Shortly after arriving in the church I formerly served, I was asked to call on a physician who was at home dying of cancer.

He sensed my uncertainty as to how to relate to him. He also didn't want his new minister to remember him only as an old man, bedfast and wasting away. So he asked me to turn on the phonograph beside his bed and play the record that was on top. I expected some quiet Brahms, or maybe even some Mozart. Instead, there suddenly burst forth a raucous version of "Sweet Georgia Brown." The doctor's eyes glowed! His wife danced beside his bed!

When it was over, he smiled kindly and said, "You didn't expect that from a dying man, did you?"

At the doctor's funeral the organist played a discreet but unmistakable rendition of "Sweet Georgia Brown."

Doctor Perham was a "grave-merry" person, one who could fly and glow even in the presence of death. He knew "God's 'heredity'" within him could "conquer the world outside" him. He knew that the awareness of God's love is the greatest gift we can receive; and, in the end, our love—conquering the evils and tragedies of the world—is the greatest gift we can give to one another. And I left his house that day "miracle lite."

Nineteen hundred years ago, the writer of 1 John put it,

> For the love of God is this, that we obey his commandments. And his commandments are not burdensome, for whatever is born of God conquers the world.

It is a faith to make you take yourself lightly, to take God's promises seriously, to treat others lovingly. It is a faith to make you "miracle lite" so you too can fly with the angels.

Amen.

> *Do not let your hearts be troubled, and do not let them be afraid.* John 14:27

Overcoming Fear

John 14:25-27

I saw a profoundly theological statement on the door of a pickup truck. Painted in Old English script, it began:

Yea though I walk through the valley of the shadow of death, I will fear no evil.

Ah, I thought, maybe a traveling evangelist. But then I continued reading:

For I am the meanest S.O.B. in the valley.

A blasphemous statement perhaps, but still a theological statement because it reveals a belief system and a way of dealing with fears.

First, let's all admit that we have some fears. Gail Sheehy, in her book *Pathfinders,* reports that

it is common for young people (those under 28) to worry about "not advancing fast enough" and to fear that "others will find out I'm not as good as they think." . . . And, among those over 45, of no longer being attractive, being abandoned, or being overtaken by illness.

Ernest Becker, in his Pulitzer Prize–winning book, *The Denial of Death,* argues that many of our fears—fear of failure, rejection, abandonment, separation, loss, sickness, and old age—are manifestations of our fear of death. Not accepting graciously the inevitability of our own mortality, we fear every sign of its proof. And surely we all do sometimes wonder about our own deaths and the deaths of loved ones, and how we will be able to cope.

The ancient Psalm 27 is evidence of the perennial presence of fear in all generations. Hear the graphic verbs used to describe the causes of fear: "assail, . . . devour, . . . stumble and fall." The psalmist then writes of finding "answerable courage," as the Pilgrims called it, in religious faith:

> The LORD is my light and my salvation;
> whom shall I fear?
> The LORD is the stronghold of my life;
> of whom shall I be afraid? (Ps. 27:1)

One of the most remarkable miracles of Jesus was his changing of the disciples from scared rabbits to lionhearted heroes, whose courage changed the world. When Peter and John were ordered with threats to cease their speaking and teaching "in the name of Jesus," they responded,

> *One of the most remarkable miracles was Jesus'*
> *changing the disciples from scared rabbits to lion-*
> *hearted heroes, whose courage changed the world.*

Whether it is right in God's sight to listen to you rather than to God, you must judge; for we cannot keep from speaking about what we have seen and heard. (Acts 4:19-20)

Such courage of the first disciples enabled the next generation to overcome their fears, even when faced with the royal madness and persecution of the Roman emperors. Tertullian, the son of a Roman centurion, a convert to Christianity in about 197 A.D., and one of early Christianity's foremost scholars, testified, "The blood of the martyrs is the seed of the Church." The survival of the Christian church through those years of sadistic suppression is indeed one of history's greatest miracles, and witness to the importance of overcoming fears.

> *The survival of the Christian church through years of sadistic suppression is, indeed, one of history's greatest miracles.*

And what I want to suggest to you now is that how we address our fears, whatever they are, has much to do with the quality of our whole lives. In her research to find out the secrets of well-being in the lives of happy people, Sheehy studied thousands of completed questionnaires and conducted hundreds of interviews over a three-year period. Her findings list ten self-descriptions as consistent characteristics of persons with a sense of optimum well-being.

1. My life is meaningful and has direction.
2. I have undergone one or more important transitions in my adult years and have handled these transitions in an unusual, personal, or creative way.
3. I rarely feel cheated or disappointed by life.
4. I have already achieved several of the long-term goals that I deem important.
5. The extent of my personal growth and development pleases me.
6. I am in love; there is mutual love between my partner and me.
7. I have many friends.
8. I am a cheerful person.
9. I am not thin-skinned or hypersensitive to criticism.
10. I have no strong fears.

Are there any common characteristics among those who say, "I have no strong fears?" Sheehy mentions two that are of particular interest to us. The first is religion.

> In every [age] group the most satisfied are also likely to be religious. Most were raised in strong religious traditions, although by mid-life they frequently had discarded dogma and repudiated religious conformity in favor of forging their own relationship to the Divine.
> For some, [faith] becomes the source of a sense of purpose. For

others, it is a secondary support that shores up the meaning and direction they feel in their lives.

Religion is optimism taken to its highest power.

Religion is one characteristic, and the other is, according to Sheehy, the willingness to take risks. In other words, rather than falling back into a defensive stance, the person with a high sense of well-being, who is not disabled by fears, starts a new journey, tries a new way. "A willingness to risk," says Sheehy, "is the master quality for pathfinding. . . . Unfortunately," she goes on, "strength is built layer by layer. Each layer is inevitably composed, at least in part, of wounds, failures, losses." And then, she says, "Even greater strength is required to ensure the scar tissue does not grow so hard over our psyche that the carapace becomes too brittle to stretch."

In short, those persons with a high sense of well-being who can say, "I have no strong fears," have two characteristics in common. They have the religious faith to trust in a gracious God who understands their needs and wants to help make things new. They have the personal strength and flexibility that gives them the courage to take risks.

> *Persons with a high sense of well-being have the religious faith to trust in a gracious God.*

And I believe those sociological findings are also in keeping with some of the basic biblical teachings about fear. In the Bible, fear is recognized as a common problem and is to be overcome as a sign of well-being.

Jesus challenges the disciples, "Do not let your hearts be troubled, and do not let them be afraid" (John 14:27). They have plenty to fear. Opposition is mounting, and, as far as they know, they are in just as much danger as Jesus. And if not physical danger, then it certainly looks like three years of their lives invested in the movement are going down the tube. They fear returning home as lonely failures, if nothing else. So, sensing their fears, Jesus challenges them by saying, according to the Phillips translation, "You must not be distressed and you must not be daunted."

Jesus felt the chill of fear himself. In the Garden of Gethsemane, his sweat, it says, "became like great drops of blood" (Luke 22:44). He prayed, "Remove this cup from me" (Luke 22:42). On the cross he screamed, "My God, my God, why have you forsaken me?" (Mark 15:34). Yet his final word was, "Father, into your hands I commend my spirit" (Luke 23:46).

It is that combination of courage and hope that was shown so beautifully in Maya Angelou's poem, "On the Pulse of Morning," read by her at the inauguration of President Clinton, in which she said "the horizon leans forward." With enough courage, she said, the pains of the past need not be repeated, for

> Each new hour holds new chances
> For a new beginning.

In the biblical tradition fear is overcome by faith in divine grace that frees one to take risks:

> The LORD is my light and my salvation;
>   whom shall I fear?
> The LORD is the stronghold of my life;
>   of whom shall I be afraid? (Ps. 27:1)

But it is also overcome by God's manifestation in human love, in the sharing with others who care. And here, I would suggest, is the uniquely Christian addition to the formula for overcoming fear.

> To love is to share ourselves with each other;
> to share the demons of our fears,
> to share the angels of our mercy;
> that by our sharing
> our demons will be diminished
> and our angels will be multiplied;
> our fears will fall and our courage will rise.

Jesus, after urging his disciples not to let their hearts be afraid, reminds them of what he had already told them, "I am going away, and I am coming to you." The spirit of Jesus will return to be with them in their hearts, to give them the courage they will need through the Spirit's presence in them. And thus they will become miracle makers in their own ways, conveying the love of Christ to others.

> *Thus they will become miracle makers in their own ways, conveying Christ's love to others.*

The First Letter of John puts it, "There is no fear in love, but perfect love casts out fear" (4:18). Howard Thurman, the great black pastor, spoke of such love in sharing with a friend in time of fear:

> I share with you the anguish of your grief,
> The anguish of your heart finds echo in my own.
> I know I cannot enter all you feel,
> Nor bear with you the burden of your pain;
> I can but offer what my love does give:
> The strength of caring,
> The warmth of one who seeks to understand
> The silent storm—swept barrenness
> of so great a loss. This I do in quiet ways,
> That on your lonely path
> You may not walk alone.*

So, three ingredients for overcoming fear, and becoming a miracle maker yourself, are:

- Faith in a gracious God who wants to help and will be with you, who leans the horizon forward.
- Courage to take risks, to be a pathfinder, confident that you just may find an even better future.
- Love to share with others both your demons and your angels, as you experience the perfect love of Christ within you. Amen.

---

*From *Deep Is the Hunger*, by Howard Thurman. © 1979 Howard Thurman. Howard Thurman Educational Trust, 2020 Stockton Street, San Francisco, CA 94133.

The Walk to Emmaus

> *They said to each other, "Were not our hearts burning within us while he was talking to us on the road, while he was opening the scriptures to us?" That same hour they got up and returned to Jerusalem. Luke 24:32-33*

Overcoming Depression

Luke 24:13-35

*H*ere is another unique Easter story, combining fantastic miracle with practical teaching. It takes place on Easter afternoon and evening, and is told only in the Gospel of Luke. Its theme, like that of the other Easter stories, is disbelief and depression, which again make the disciples almost miss the meaning of Jesus' resurrection for their lives.

> *The disciples almost miss the meaning of Jesus' resurrection for their lives.*

In this story two disciples, one named Cleopas and the other unnamed, have left Jerusalem. They've had enough of the bad news there: the betrayals, the denials, the distortions, the dreams dashed. Suckers they were, even to have hoped for so much. On the fight or flight scale of human response to crisis, the fight has been taken out of them by what has happened in the city. Flight is the answer now that Jesus is dead. And so they put their backs to Jerusalem and head for

83

Emmaus, a quiet village about seven miles away. It is while they are walking and talking together about what has happened, so the story goes, that the resurrected "Jesus himself came near and went with them." So depressed are they, however, that they don't even recognize him. "They stood still, looking sad," Luke says. Phillips translates it, "They stopped, their faces drawn with misery."

Again, it is easy to see why they are so depressed and disabled. It seems that everything has gone wrong. Jesus is dead. The movement is ended. Their dreams are buried. Their hopes are entombed. The flesh of love has been punched through and hung up by nails on a cross. The only person they ever met who truly could be called "the Child of God" has been betrayed and denied by those he thought were his friends, then cursed, stripped, beaten, spit upon, and mocked as he died.

They had thought that after years of struggle they were finally set to enjoy the rest of their lives. With Jesus as King, they would sit in positions of honor and comfort. Instead, it's back to "Go," with the penalties of grief and disillusionment added.

So of course they are depressed as they trudge the seven miles to Emmaus, "their faces drawn with misery." Of course they are so spiritually disabled that they don't recognize Jesus when he joins them.

But in the end it is a story offering three antidotes to depression and disablement. The first antidote, I would suggest to you, is the antidote of Christian realism.

When the "stranger" joins them and asks why they look so terrible and are so depressed, Cleopas and his friend recount the awful things that have happened, adding, "We had hoped that he was the one to redeem Israel." Hope is now past tense! To which Jesus replies: "Oh, how foolish you are, and how slow of heart to believe all that the prophets have declared! Was it not necessary that the Messiah should suffer these things and then enter into his glory?"

What the resurrected Christ, whom they still don't recognize, is saying is: Where have you been? How simplistic can you be? Don't you know even yet what to expect from human nature? Do you think you or anyone is exempt from life's failures, injustices, wrongs, and tragedies? Who promised you a rose garden? Look back even at our faith history. Abraham was a liar, and sent Sarah, his wife, to

84

Pharaoh's bed to save his own skin. Jacob was a thief who cheated his brother, Esau, his father, Isaac, and his father-in-law, Laban. Moses murdered an Egyptian. King David got the hots for Bathsheba. Later when he found that she was pregnant, he had her husband Uriah killed.

Perhaps Jesus reminded them of his own teachings about realism: "See, I am sending you out like sheep into the midst of wolves; So be wise as serpents and innocent as doves" (Matt. 10:16).

Probably he recalled how he had told them, though in their naive underestimate of the potential for evil people have they didn't believe him, that he would be killed.

Yes, the first antidote is realism. Mark Twain called it being human: "All that I care to know is that a man is a human being—that is enough for me; he can't be any worse." And "Man is the only animal that blushes. Or needs to."

In terms of the general human condition, the Bible calls it sin and says don't act so surprised or so self-righteous when you see its results. Accept its reality as a part of being human, not as an aberration. Then, maybe, you will deal with it, rather than just complain about it. That's the reason for keeping the evil of the Holocaust alive in the social conscience. Elie Wiesel said at the dedication of the Holocaust Memorial museum in Washington, D.C., "What have we learned? . . . We have learned that we are all responsible, that indifference is a sin." Vice President Al Gore asked, "What terrible darkness lies coiled in the human soul that might account for this barbarism?"

Also accept the reality of sin in yourself. "If we say we have no sin, we deceive ourselves, and the truth is not in us" (1 John 1:8 RSV). Admit that there will probably never be a day in your life when you will not live with it in some form, and that it will only increase with your naive trust in its absence.

Another way to put it is this: Expect that some awful things are going to happen, for whatever cause, even on your own life journey. No one is exempt. The rain shall fall "on the just and on the unjust" (Matt. 5:45). It is the price of our God-given freedom, which most of us would prefer, even to benevolent control.

> *Expect that some awful things are going to happen on your life journey.*

The wife of a man with cancer said, "It doesn't seem fair. I wish we could be guaranteed ninety good years; then let anything happen!"

How well I understand that longing, born of deep human love that dreads the pain and parting of a beloved. But when I shared it with another woman, whose husband also has cancer, she replied, "And if we were guaranteed ninety, then we would want a hundred."

One of the antidotes from the Emmaus Road story is the acceptance of the fact that we all live in a grief-tainted world, where none—not even Christ—escapes its tragic touch.

But now comes the Easter gospel: That is not all. The grief of human realism is not the whole story. For what the story also says is that the resurrected Christ joins the two disciples on the road and walks with them. They don't recognize him at first. That's a subtle reminder, as in all the Easter stories, that it is not the physics, but the Spirit of Easter that matters. In other words: On their depressing, failed, fear-filled road, they do not walk alone. The divine Spirit, the risen Christ, walks, step-by-step, beside them.

> *The divine Spirit, the risen Christ, walks, step-by-step, beside them.*

Psalm 23 offers the same message:

Yea, though I walk through the valley of the shadow of death, I will fear no evil: for thou art with me. (v. 4 KJV)

Or as William Law put it:

Thou canst not fall below the arms of God, howsoever low thou fallest.

But, you ask, "How does the resurrected Christ walk with us? I haven't seen him on my Emmaus roads." Nor did the first disciples recognize him. That's the point! All they saw was a friend, who walked with them and tried both to comfort their hearts and to challenge their minds.

How does Christ walk with us on our Emmaus roads?

How does Christ walk with us on our Emmaus roads? His presence may be in a friend who will simply walk with us and share our heart's pain. This is the second antidote, filling the heart's longing for supportive companionship. It is what James Baldwin meant when he wrote, "The moment we cease to hold each other, the moment we break faith with one another, the sea engulfs us and the light goes out."

But let's face it, there are many times when even that is not enough. When more than sharing and companionship are needed. When too much sympathy from a friend actually becomes harmful. In modern terms that is called enabling: When even your well-intended sympathy or tolerance enables another person to continue destructive behavior, rather than admit that changes need to be made, and then to make them.

In other words, more than sympathy from others is needed in recovering from life's tragedies and depressions. Equally needed is personal action. And that's what I read into the exclamation and action of the two disciples near the end of the story.

The three of them have arrived at Emmaus at the end of the seven-mile walk. Being evening, they eat together. It is when Jesus says a blessing and breaks the bread, Luke says, that "their eyes were opened, and they recognized him." With that, Jesus disappears, vanishes. And the disciples say to one another, "Were not our hearts burning within us while he was talking to us on the road, while he was opening the scriptures to us?"

Do you get it? Hearts and minds both had to be involved: Yes, the explanation of the reality of human sin for their minds; yes, sympathetic companionship for their hearts. But now that they have intellectual understanding and supportive friendship, one more antidote for their depression is needed: their personal action. "That same hour they got up and returned to Jerusalem."

The Phillips translation says, "They got to their feet without delay and turned back."

First came the acceptance of the reality of human sin; second, supportive friendship; and third, personal action.

A career management consultant spoke recently to our Ministerial Association. His topic was "Helping People Who Have Lost Their Jobs." His presentation had five main points:

1. Understand the Job Loss Reaction Cycle.
2. Be Supportive—But Don't Coddle.
3. Provide the Right Kind of Support Groups (not Pity Parties).
4. Focus on Strengths.
5. The Best Strategy Is to Use Several Strategies.

From acceptance of reality, to supportive friendship, to personal action. Finally, to get a new job, one has to leave the support group and "hit the streets."

And that's the way this Bible story ends. "That same hour they got up and returned to Jerusalem." Finding the rest of the disciples, they tell them what has happened, and all exclaim, "The Lord has risen indeed!"

Like tired turtles they had left; like racing rabbits (like Easter rabbits, filled with "hop") they returned. Running the entire seven miles back, even though it was now dark, they made one of history's fastest U-turns from depression to action. Their story started, "They stood still, looking sad." Their old story ended and their new story began, "They got up and returned." They were resurrected! They became Easters! They were miracles, and all the disciples said, "The Lord has risen indeed!"

It is a charming old story, and with lessons writ large, I think, for us. It was also a source of inspiration and strength for the early Christians. When Stephen was stoned to death, Jerusalem destroyed, and the church persecuted, life's tragedies didn't seem quite so final, because Christians had three antidotes for depression:

1. the acceptance of the reality of human sin
2. participation in supportive friendships
3. personal action for the future

and belief in a God of continuing resurrections, which could still make their hearts "burn within them." Amen.

And not only that, but we also boast in our sufferings, knowing that suffering produces endurance, and endurance produces character, and character produces hope, and hope does not disappoint us, because God's love has been poured into our hearts through the Holy Spirit that has been given to us. Rom. 5:3-5

When Miracles Fail

Romans 5:1-11

Paul has a problem.

It's the problem of human suffering.

He wants Christianity to continue growing. But he has to admit that it doesn't seem to end personal suffering. If he could pull off such a miracle, it would be very good for publicity. Unfortunately, miracles of healing such as Jesus performed are not in Paul's considerable array of spiritual gifts.

This letter is written to the Christians in Rome. Ten years later Paul himself will be decapitated there, on orders from Emperor Nero.

Even when writing this letter, at the height of his influence in about the year 57, Paul speaks of his "thorn in the flesh." No one knows what it was: a physical ailment—some have suggested epilepsy, given his "seizure" on the Damascus Road; an emotional imbalance—his writing may well suggest that he was manic-depressive; or was it some moral lapse, causing a guilt that continued to haunt him?

Three times I appealed to the Lord about this, that it would leave me, but he said to me, "My grace is sufficient for you, for power is made perfect in weakness." (2 Cor. 12:8-9)

In other words, the thorn is not going to be removed. To be a Christian does not mean being exempt from suffering. It does mean using suffering to grow in the experience of God's grace and power.

> *To be a Christian does not mean being exempt from suffering.*

And so Paul writes here to the Christians in Rome:

And not only that, but we also boast in our sufferings, knowing that suffering produces endurance, and endurance produces character, and character produces hope, and hope does not disappoint us, because God's love has been poured into our hearts through the Holy Spirit that has been given to us.

The thesis of this sermon is this: No one is exempt from suffering. But when miracles of healing seem to fail, there is another miracle of God's grace that can be experienced through the gift of God's love in our hearts.

> *When miracles of healing seem to fail, there is another miracle of God's grace that can be experienced through the gift of God's love in our hearts.*

In short, suffering, as Paul says, may produce endurance, character, and hope *if* it serves to release the love of God which has been "poured into our hearts." And when that happens it truly can be called a miracle of grace.

No one is exempt from suffering. Bob Witzeman was my best friend. We grew up together. From the first grade on we shared an unusually large number of the same experiences.

- For twelve years we were always in the same classes at school.
- Our families attended the same church.
- We went to the same Sunday school, summer camps, and youth conferences.
- We were confirmed together and sang in the same choir.
- As young teenagers, we both worked after school and on Saturdays as stock boys in the same dime store.
- In high school, Bob was elected president of our sophomore class, and I of our junior class.
- In our senior year, we were in the same honor societies, and both even earned our letters on the football team, where he was quarterback, and I was a skinny 125-pound end.

We had long talks about the future, and both decided during our junior year of high school that we wanted to go to college and then study for the ministry.

One helpful family in our church even took us to visit the same college. Bob decided to go to another, so our ways were—for the first time in twelve years—parted for a while.

Still, we saw each other during the summers in our hometown, where we returned for summer jobs. And a highlight of those hot, lazy Indiana summer days was the long evenings of tennis (we must have played thousands of games), swapping stories and dreams of the future.

Graduating the same year from separate colleges, we decided to go to the same seminary for theological studies.

My wife to be, Donna, was also a student there, and I soon found that Bob cared for her almost as much as I did. He lost that one, though! And, being a fine organist, ended up playing for our wedding.

We would have finished seminary and probably have been ordained together in our home church, had Bob not taken a year out to work in a Church World Service Camp, helping to rebuild Germany.

Returning from Germany, and ready for his final year of seminary, Bob came to visit Donna and me in early September, now in another little Indiana town, beginning our first ministry. And he was pleased and fascinated as we were that Donna was now becoming large with our first child.

For the Christmas holiday that year, Bob felt fortunate to land a job as a temporary mail deliverer in our hometown.

But it was to be his last.

A few days after Christmas we received one of those dreaded telephone calls. Bob was in the hospital. He had cancer of the blood—leukemia. They were trying to change his blood. But he might not make it. Before I could get there—Donna was too near delivery to travel—Bob died.

Standing by Bob's casket over that open grave, in the cemetery where we had so often ridden our bicycles together, was one of the few times in my life that I have really sobbed.

I sobbed at the personal loss of my best buddy.

I sobbed at the world's loss of his blossoming intellect, artistry, and generosity.

I sobbed at my own faith-confusion. If God is so powerful, and if God is so good, then why are such things allowed to happen?

Not able to say it was the will of God, as some said, and not pretending to know the answer, Donna and I, instinctively, still wanted somehow to declare our faith rather than our bitterness. So, two weeks later, when our first son was born, we named him "Robert" (Bob), as a sign of our love and hope.

Some say it is the most perplexing faith question of all. "Why do so many bad things happen to so many good people?" "Why, if God is so good, doesn't God fix things that break?" "Why, if God is so powerful, does God allow things to break in the first place?"

Humorist Ogden Nash expressed his frustration in a couplet:

> The Lord in his wisdom made the fly,
> And then forgot to tell us why.

Joseph Heller, in his zany but brilliant novel *Catch-22,* has Yossarian exclaim:

> "Good God, how much reverence can you have for a Supreme Being who finds it necessary to include tooth decay in His divine system of creation? Why in the world did He ever create pain?"
>
> "Pain?" Lieutenant Shiesskopf's wife pounced upon the word victoriously. "Pain is a useful symptom. Pain is a warning to us of bodily dangers."
>
> "And who created the dangers?" Yossarian demanded. "Why couldn't God have used a doorbell to notify us, or one of His celestial

choirs? Or a system of blue-and-red neon tubes right in the middle of each person's forehead?"

"People would certainly look silly walking around with red neon tubes in the middle of their foreheads."

"They certainly look beautiful now writhing in agony, don't they?"

Human suffering is a reality, in spite of human virtue.

You don't have to tell that to the parents of a little baby girl born with a heart defect that requires surgery.

You don't have to tell that to the parents of a teenage boy killed in an automobile accident.

You don't have to tell that to the parents of a young adult who is gay in a homophobic society, and now has AIDS.

You don't have to tell that to a wife whose beloved husband dies in midlife when his heart can pump no more.

And what is the gospel to these people, and hundreds more with other sufferings, in body, mind, and soul, just in this congregation? Well personally, I'm going to go light on Paul's counsel about "suffering produces endurance, and endurance produces character, and character produces hope. Therefore, we boast (or rejoice) in our sufferings."

In my experience, endurance and character and hope *may* be increased in the long run by suffering.

> *Endurance, character, and hope may be increased in the long run by suffering.*

But that is not the starting place. It may even be cruel counsel, heaping even more burden on someone who already feels so inadequate, and nearly broken with fear or grief. In my experience, what one really needs in times of suffering is

> not a push, but an embrace,
> not pressure, but compassion,
> not a pep talk, but a prayer,
> not an exhortation, but a hug,
> not explanation, but love.

94

And that, I think, is what Paul is really saying too. If suffering is to be used for growth in endurance, character, and hope, it will be a by-product of the first requirement. And that requirement, as Paul says, is gracious love.

Why is it possible that suffering might produce endurance, character, and hope? "Because," Paul writes, "God's love has been poured into our hearts." And, "The Lord . . . said to me, 'My grace is sufficient for you.'"

The eleven-year-old son of very dear friends in our former church died within weeks of being diagnosed with aplastic anemia. Ten years later the mother wrote me about the terrible grief that she and her husband had to work through, the bitterness they had to overcome.

"I can truly say now that loving is a way of being in the world where there are no answers to some of our deepest questions. And, it feels good to be able to say it."

Not arguments, but empathy.

Not answers, but love.

Gracious love "is sufficient"; the sufficient starting place, if sufferings are ultimately to produce that noble growth in endurance, character, and hope. If ever we really are to "boast (or rejoice) in our sufferings," the ability to keep loving after "miracles fail" is indeed another miracle of God's grace.

> *The ability to keep loving after "miracles fail" is indeed another miracle of God's grace.*

Archibald MacLeish's play *J.B.* is a modern telling of the story of Job. Job and Sarah have lost nearly everything. Their oldest son has been killed in war. Their one daughter has been raped and murdered. Two teenage children have died in an automobile crash, and another has been crushed by stones. Their business has failed, and so has Job's health. Now their house and town have been demolished by a tornadic holocaust. In the final scene, the stage direction says:

They cling to each other. Then she rises, drawing him up, peering at the darkness inside the door.

J.B.: It's too dark to see.

She turns, pulls his head down between her hands and kisses him.

Sarah: Then blow on the coal of the heart, my darling.
J.B.: The coal of the heart . . .
Sarah: It's all the light now.

And then, as the play ends,

Sarah comes forward into the dim room, J.B. behind her. She lifts a fallen chair, sets it straight.

[Sarah:] Blow on the coal of the heart.
The candles in churches are out.
The lights have gone out in the sky.
Blow on the coal of the heart
And we'll see by and by . . .

J.B. has joined her, lifting and straightening the chairs.

We'll see where we are.
The wit won't burn and the wet soul smoulders.
Blow on the coal of the heart and we'll know . . .
We'll know . . .*

In times of suffering,

- we, in love, are to blow on the coals of each other's hearts;
- the church, in love, is to blow on the heart of the world;

so souls and societies that have become wet with tears will smolder eventually into what was meant to be. Amen.
